"As a first time author Wendy challenges us to let go of our 'supposed to be's' and accept 'realities' through her personal story of loss and healing. She offers wisdom, biblical learning and the reframing of hope, all while nudging us to her discovery of God's providence in her life. Reading this book, I smiled, teared up and often thought, 'I've found someone just like me within the pages of her journal, and it feels good!' Her book is a warm journey well worth walking through to guide you on your own becoming through suffering."

- Rob A., Orillia, ON

"I didn't see that coming! Perhaps you have at some point been upended by an unexpected occurrence that mushroomed into an all consuming stress-filled reality. Such was my experience. At that time, I was deeply grateful to read Wendy Stanley's honest account of how she journeyed with God through a traumatic experience. Whatever your trauma, you will benefit greatly when you walk through this wonderful, interactive book with God who loves you and desires His good will for your life."

- Alison C., Mt. Forest, ON

"Wendy's story stopped me in my tracks. As I read the book, chapter by chapter, I kept thinking: I can relate to this topic; I've been in this very place; I know these struggles. As I carefully considered the questions at the end of each chapter, buried truth was revealed to me. It was time to let Jesus do a deeper work in me."

- Donna J., Owen Sound, ON

D1720036

I DIDN'T SEE THAT COMING

EXPERIENCING THE SHEPHERD HEART OF GOD WHEN LIFE HURTS UNEXPECTEDLY

WENDY G. STANLEY

WD
PUBLISHING HOUSE ✄

CONTENTS

INTRODUCTION

It wasn't that long ago when life as I knew it abruptly and unexpectedly changed. It was as if, for a moment in time, my world stopped. Just one mis-step significantly impacted my life and continues to influence me today. This is my story, a story of a hard season in life that turned into one of the greatest challenges and blessings I've ever experienced.

Shortly after moving to a new community, experiencing an empty nest for the first time, and struggling with how to live a new pace of life, I severely broke my ankle. I suddenly found myself in a season of deep pain and suffering, not only physically, but emotionally and spiritually as well.

I was completely unprepared for what happened, what would come next, or how long it would take to recover. The depth of grief, pain, weakness, loss and alone-ness I felt was far beyond what I ever could have anticipated. While the season of sudden suffering was one of the hardest times in my life, it also came with some wonderful blessings. Through the valley, I was able to hear God's voice more clearly than I ever have. I learned to appreciate the simple things in life like I never had before. Furthermore, the sudden difficulty has been the catalyst to tremendous spiritual growth, emotional maturity, and a whole new understanding of physical pain and health.

My season of suffering led to an entirely new way of life for me. How the Lord supplied for me and my family in tangible and spiritual ways has been exceedingly good, even profound at times. This experience has so significantly changed me that I feel compelled to tell others about it.

The following line from the song "My Story" by Big Daddy Weave encapsulates my intention with this book:

"Oh, to tell you my story is to tell of Him."

The "Him" here refers to God, the Father of our Lord Jesus Christ. Jesus Christ has brought me from emotional and physical brokenness to a place of mental, emotional, spiritual, and physical healing. For that reason, I can't keep silent. I feel like a different person! Critical areas in my life have been re-made. Until this all happened, I didn't know that those areas needed changing.

My journey of healing and strengthening has been filled with unexpected benefits and blessings, as well as a great deal of pain and grief. Who knew that falling on my butt would be life changing in a good way? When my ankle shattered, many of my preconceived notions would shatter also, although not as quickly! My thinking needed to change. It needed to be re-aligned and re-built to God's way of looking at things.

While I could chronologically unpack my journey and recount it in a diary of sorts, I have found that most people are interested in what I've learned along the way. Even though this isn't a diary, I have chosen some entries from my journal to share my thoughts and emotions at the time. I will reveal the raw reality of what I went through and how Jesus Christ sustained me.

Each chapter shares a lesson or a new thought I'm learning to live out. These lessons are not only for me, and that's why I'm writing this book. I had no idea that I'd be writing a book about this experience, but I believe God placed it on my heart two months after my accident. The thought of writing a book just wouldn't go away. Over several weeks, snappy one liners popped into my mind during the day and in the night. I began to write them down and they have become the chapter titles. The title of the book came to me in the same way.

My story and experience is unique to me. After years of living a life of busyness, I became completely immobile, in a place where I knew no one, at a time when I was alone for what felt like hours on end. However, I believe that the lessons and truths that follow can apply to anyone who has experienced a major trauma or sudden shift in their lives.

We all have different struggles, difficulties, and challenges in life. We can learn so much in any situation when life as we know it pivots so suddenly, our head spins. I trust that what I've been learning can help others who are also experiencing suffering.

The Bible talks about suffering a great deal. Jesus told His disciples that they would have tribulation while living in the world (see John 16:33). That word "tribulation" means trouble, or affliction of any kind. Neither trouble nor suffering is fun. When it happens, we question God. We wonder how things could have been different had God intervened. We struggle to try to understand why it happened, or what we did to deserve what is happening to us.

There were times I thought these things. I asked, "Where were my guardian angels? Why hadn't they caught my foot, and protected my fall? Why did I have to break my ankle so violently and dramatically? A bad sprain or a simple break would have been so much easier." Having surgery to install a long plate and numerous screws seemed to be a little extreme in my opinion.

The truth is, I have no idea why it happened. I do know, however, that it has been one of the best things that happened to me. That sounds very strange, but it's true. I'm thankful for the difficulty I experienced. Not because I enjoy pain, because I most certainly do not! But the things I have learned through the difficulty, and the closeness I felt to God in that time, are things I will never forget.

Even more so, the fact that it happened in an unfamiliar place where I had virtually no support, became the condition for me to lean most heavily on Jesus Christ rather than on myself or people.

In the pages of this book, I'm going to give an account of the journey of my accident, my recovery, and all the things I have come to understand about God, myself, and others. I am writing out of a desire to obey the Lord and impart the things that God can do in the middle of particularly difficult situations. It is my desire to encourage others to know that they too can experience the goodness of God regardless of what they are going through right now. I hope that what I am sharing from my life will help you. It's good to know that we're not alone, we will get through it, and that God will comfort, provide, and sustain us as we walk through the valleys in life.

I have organized this book in such a way that you can read it from the beginning, or choose the chapters that have the most relevance or interest to you. Each chapter has three questions for you to further contemplate the content of the book and to self-examine your own hard seasons of life.

It is my prayer that you will find healing, comfort, hope, and joy through these pages. We have a very personal God who desires a personal and intimate relationship with us. Do you know Him?

ONE

THE BACK STORY

In order to move forward through life, it is often helpful to look back from time to time. It's in recalling the past that we can see how far we have come. More importantly, we can better understand why we reacted in certain ways to the various joys and sorrows of life. This chapter is my "back story", an overview of life prior to what I call my "sudden suffering".

I would like to provide the context as to why I found my significantly broken ankle to be such a life crisis. In and of itself, a broken ankle heals, and people move on, but in my case, there were some additional challenges I was facing that contributed to a wholly difficult season. The physical trauma of my displaced ankle became the proverbial straw that broke the camel's back, and led me to a crisis of faith, a re-orientation of my theology, and a profound time of maturing, both emotionally and spiritually. Not to mention, my broken ankle has been an on-going physical challenge to me longer than I ever expected!

The best word I can use to describe my life up to six months prior to my shattering experience would have to be "busy" with a capital "B"! I was firing on all cylinders most of the time. Here's what I mean:

- Our youngest son, Charles lived at home. He was completing his final year of high school and preparing for university in the fall. Every parent's role differs at this stage in their child's life, but mine was coach, cheerleader, and encourager (perhaps a bit of a pusher too).

- I was chief cook, cleaner, launderer, grocery shopper, banker, and organizer for Charles and my husband, Derek, who worked full time and was often away from home in the evenings, and occasionally overnight.

- We owned two income properties, one in Owen Sound where we lived, and another sixty minutes away. The out of town property required weekly visits. I was the main contact person for the tenants, and I was responsible for all aspects of property management.

- Derek and I hosted and co-led "house church" two evenings a week.

- Another evening a week, I was involved in the

local Celebrate Recovery group. In fact, I was one of the main leaders, responsible for many parts of the ministry, including teaching weekly lessons, overall administration, training new leaders, and sponsoring individuals on their recovery journey, as well as working on my own recovery.

- I was a very social person, maintaining friendships with a wide circle of individuals, which included regular coffees, breakfasts, lunches, and walks, etc.
- My aging parents lived three hours away in Toronto, and I had been making an effort to visit them more often.

My life was "go-go-go" most of the time. That is, until Derek and I decided to move to Mount (Mt.) Forest. Not only would this move result in us being an hour closer to my parents and Charles, who was accepted to the University of Guelph, but it would also save Derek up to eight hours of driving a week! To us, that was significant enough to make the move.

We made the decision quickly, choosing a thirty day closing date, and taking advantage of having our sons, Derek Jr. and Charles at home to help us. We moved at the end of August, just prior to their starting the new university year. The speed at which we moved upset the apple cart in some of our closest relationships. It was a shock to several of our friends.

Shock number one for me occurred when we packed

up the truck and moved to Mt. Forest on August 30, 2019. I went from a highly active, purpose-filled, friend-rich life, with a family at home, to an empty nest, not knowing one soul, and to almost zero activity, other than setting up a new home.

The emotional toll this had on me was profound. I was immediately launched into a season of grief and loss. The empty nest experience was very hard for me as I had been a stay at home mom for all of my children's years prior to their leaving for university. I think my identity was wrapped up in being a mom, plus I was fearful of the temptations Charles would face. Derek Jr. had been away for a year in Ottawa, six and a half hours away, and I also dearly missed him.

Having lived in Owen Sound for seven years, and the Grey-Bruce area for over twenty, we had a wide range of friends and connections that we were leaving behind. Even though our move was only an hour away, it seemed like a million miles to some of our friends.

I experienced a deep sense of loneliness from being without friends, some of whom weren't happy with me. I found myself confused and unsure what to do with my time. I suddenly had a lot of it, which was new for me. I did some painting, walking, gardening, talking to the Lord, and visiting my family; and I enjoyed the sense of having no on-going commitments or obligations. Yet, it was also incredibly strange and discombobulating. Here are some of my journal entries at that time:

Father, I see how restless I am. My flesh is screaming for relief – I do not like being alone. I don't like not being needed. I feel like I'm not doing anything. I feel alone, useless, and unimportant. My flesh fights against rest. Oh Lord, deliver me! Who can't enjoy the relaxed life? I sure don't understand that.

(Journal, November 8, 2019)

Oh Father, I'm grieving – loss on multiple fronts, and yet there's good things too. I'm needing your comforting arms around me. Sometimes I just feel so alone and out of sorts.

(Journal, November 18, 2019)

In the first three months of living in Mt. Forest, there were a few activities I got involved in. Derek and I attended a local church, and had signed up for a weekly Bible study starting in late October. In mid November, I joined the local Pickleball league, which ran a few times a week. My intention, beyond it being a healthy activity, was to make some friends. By this time, I had enjoyed a coffee with one person from the church, and once I had chatted over the fence with our next door neighbour. This was a good start, but it was still very early days.

In late October, an opportunity for us to purchase an income property seemed to drop into our laps. We had been looking for a few months already. We pursued this one because it was exactly what we had been looking for. On November 29, 2019, Derek and I were the new owners of an eight plex in Hanover, a thirty five minute drive from Mt. Forest.

At that point, I would return to work-mode as landlord to seven tenants, and property manager for the building. I would need to go through the process of filling an apartment, and Derek and I were going to completely overhaul that empty apartment. It needed paint of course, but also new flooring and counter tops, a new fridge, and a solution to a very ugly and dirty bathtub. The whole apartment was a disaster, entirely disgusting, and in desperate need of elbow grease and upgrades.

Suddenly my life would become more active, and with Pickleball and church, the opportunity to make friends was beginning. I wouldn't be traveling to Owen Sound as much. In the first two months of moving, I had needed to go to Owen Sound to check on our home which hadn't sold yet. While I did that, I also visited numerous friends, to maintain connection. But by mid November, the deal had closed.

Shock number two is the catalyst to this book. The title "I didn't see that coming" truly illustrates the reality in my life. On December 2, 2019, just three days after taking ownership of our new property, making a few new connections in Mt. Forest, starting a Bible study, and playing Pickleball several times a week, I severely broke my ankle. This resulted in a distinct and disruptive change to my burgeoning new life.

Immediately, I had to stop everything. The opportunities for connection stopped. My ability to go anywhere stopped. My sport and mobility stopped. My independence stopped. In one moment in time. On one day.

QUESTIONS:

1. Describe a time in your life when you had a major shock, and were thrown into a time of sudden suffering.

2. We all react to our trials and troubles in different ways. Looking back, think about the ways you responded to your seasons of suffering. How did your flesh scream for relief?

3. In what ways can you relate to Wendy's life, emotions, or story?

TWO

IT WAS JUST ANOTHER DAY

On Monday morning, December 2, 2019, I woke up, showered, and got ready for Pickleball, an activity I had just started. Since I didn't know anyone in town, I saw this as an opportunity to get some exercise, have fun, and maybe make a new friend. It was a cold and sunny morning.

When I arrived at the old arena in town, the five Pickleball courts were set up and several people were already there. The courts were on the surface of the old hockey arena, which meant the floor could be slippery, and the air quite chilly at times. It was both of those things that day. Some of the other players were wearing their gloves and winter coats. Anticipating a fun time, I got onto a court quickly.

The game of Pickleball is a combination of tennis, ping pong, and badminton. The equipment includes a racquetball racket and a wiffle ball. It is most often played with two players on each side of the court. When I was in my teens and early twenties, I played badminton and tennis frequently, and I've always loved ping pong. I took to it fairly easily. Mind you, that didn't mean I was good. I had a lot to learn because the rules were different, the court was much smaller, and that wiffle ball sure behaved differently than a tennis ball!

I really enjoyed this new sport after playing only a few times. I loved running around, laughing at myself, learning something new, and meeting new people. I think that day was my fifth time playing. I wore my brand new running shoes so as not to slide on the floor. I had already fallen - basically somersaulted - once or twice before because of the poor traction on my older shoes. I expected the new ones to give me better grip. Not to mention, on several occasions, the ladies had said, "No ball is worth a fall". They were quite concerned about safety, since in the past year, at least one person had fallen and badly injured themselves.

The nice thing I discovered about this Pickleball league was that it was mainly for fun. Nobody kept a running total of wins or losses. In addition, there were no tournaments or trophies. Everyone simply rotated who they played with, based on whether they had won or lost their last game. This gave me the opportunity to play with different men and women, each at varying skill levels. Even though it was mainly for fun, I confess, like any sport, winning is the object of the game. I've always had a rather competitive spirit, so that day was no different. My partner and I were trying to win as much as our opponents were.

It was our first game of the day. My partner and I were already down five points to zero; okay, maybe more, but who's counting? The other side served, my partner returned, and I moved up to the line behind "the kitchen". This "kitchen" spot was an important position, one I had just started playing. I had to learn to stand close to the net, but not as close as in tennis. Our opponents returned the ball, which flew high, just a little over my head.

In tennis, when the ball goes high, it's a great opportunity for a smash. That was my plan. I jumped up as high as my short legs would go in an effort to strike the ball down, making it hard for my opponents to return it. The goal was that we would win the serve, and have the opportunity to score some points.

The ball went out of bounds, and as I came down from my jump, which seemed to be very slowly, I landed on the floor. Unfortunately, I didn't land on my feet like a cat. I landed with a splat. Actually, it was more like a crumpled heap. The first point of contact with the floor was the outside of my left ankle, followed by the rest of my body. Not too gracefully I might add. The pain in my ankle was instant and overwhelming. All I could say was, "It hurts. Oh, it hurts.", as I writhed around on the cold, hard floor.

Immediately, from our opponents' side, one of the ladies ran over to me, put her hands under my leg, and held up my foot. I soon learned she was a nurse. She took a peek at my ankle, asked the other players for their coats, and told another lady to run for the ice packs. She also told someone to call 911. She knew the injury was bad. Another lady quickly came around to hold my head on her lap. Maybe she was a nurse too; she knew exactly what to do for me.

Several of the other players placed their coats under my body, which was good; the floor was cold and I was now shivering. I felt the ice packs being placed around my ankle, and I heard the nurse instructing me how to breathe so that I wouldn't hyperventilate. I was also asked, "Are you dizzy?", "Are you nauseous?", "Are you comfortable?", and "Would you like me to hold your head higher?" I don't know how long it all took.

All I knew was that this was the worst pain I've ever felt in my life. Over and over I was reminded to breathe in through my nose and out through my mouth, and to breathe deeply. In those early moments, with the pain and shock, I might have actually forgotten how to breathe properly.

To be lying on the floor like that was a complete surprise to me, and the pain was so bad! Looking back, I don't doubt that I was in shock, pain, and utter confusion. I was also embarrassed, and rather inconvenienced.

As we waited for the paramedics to arrive, I was asked, "Where's your coat? Where's your purse? Where's your car?", and "What's your husband's phone number?" I also noticed the other players around me, most of whom had concern and sadness written all over their faces. I felt quite badly for them because my accident had interrupted their Pickleball games. After all, they had come to have fun and get exercise that day too!

When the two paramedics arrived, they went into action very quickly. First, they cut my pants - down the seam - after I told them that they were my favourite pair. Next, the laces on my brand new shoes were cut. After that, I'm not entirely sure what happened except that I was given many forms of painkillers. Pills by mouth, a sweet juice, and possibly a pain medication by injection - all these were administered to me while I lay on the many coats on the cold, hard floor of the arena.

My ankle was resting on a pillow or something the paramedics had placed under it, and my shoulders and back still rested on someone else's knees. At this point, I started to feel the cold floor. Sadly, I didn't experience much change in the pain. I was breathing better though, and I definitely felt well cared for.

The entire time this was happening, I was thinking:

"This had better be a sprain.

I can't afford to have a break.

It has to be a sprain.

It can't be a break.

I did not hear a crack.

I did not break my bone."

Why was I so adamant that it had better not be a break? The main reason was that Derek and I were just starting the renovation process of one of our apartments in our new apartment building. It was on the top floor, which was five flights up with no elevator. We had spent no more than five hours cleaning, and we still had a great deal more to do before that was finished, let alone the painting, new flooring, etc. Add to that the fact that Christmas was coming in just over three weeks, and I hadn't even started shopping. Plus, I had just started playing this new sport, and I was really enjoying it!

The paramedics didn't want to move me onto the stretcher until my pain was under control, so they continued to minister to me and prepare for transport. This took some time. Finally, when the pain had subsided somewhat, the paramedics helped me to stand up on my good foot. They held me under my arm pits while two of the men from Pickleball held the stretcher steady.

Supported by the paramedics, I hopped a few steps over to the stretcher. Then I got my behind up onto the stretcher, and shimmied along until I was fully on it, with my legs straight out. As I write these words, I have to giggle. Doing that shimmy movement on my rear end would be something I would do a lot of in the days and months ahead.

One end of the stretcher was lifted, and I was able to

sit up. Everyone was standing around watching me, and I thought, "Darn! I was just getting started at this." As the paramedics wheeled me out, there were other players lined up along the walls of the inner hallway. When I passed by them, I put my hand up into the air, and cried out, "If you pray, pray it's a sprain. Not a break!"

Once I was in the ambulance, I started to panic. I may even have started to hyperventilate. Perhaps the shock was kicking in more, or maybe it was the anxiety from never having ridden in an ambulance. After all, a sprain wouldn't necessarily put someone in an ambulance, would it?

The paramedic sitting in the back with me reminded me how to breathe, and got me talking. She asked about my family and whatever would get my mind off my current situation. The ride was quick – the hospital is only five minutes away – and the medications were starting to take effect. I said to the driver, "Can we go around the block? This is my first ride in an ambulance."

When we arrived at the hospital, I was parked in the hallway near the door. Every time the door swished opened, a draft of icy cold air rushed in, meaning that I couldn't get warm, even with the many heated blankets the paramedics had given me. I was shivering a lot. What I understand now is that the shivering could have been from the cold, and it could have been from the trauma that my body was experiencing.

Thankfully, the pain medications kicked in enough that

I wasn't so focused on the pain. Instead, I began to crack jokes with the paramedics. What a strange response! One of the paramedics commented on how she finds it funny watching people when the pain medications are working, because they can get pretty silly. I know I certainly did.

It wasn't long after I arrived at the hospital that I saw a friendly face - my husband Derek. Derek is not the type to coddle me or hold my hand in an effort to take away pain or bring comfort. Instead, he cracked a joke. He said, "Well, you've got yourself in a pickle now, haven't you?"

I think somehow he knew that what had happened wasn't good, that not only was this going to affect my life dramatically, but it was going to change his life as well. The hospital hallway was cold, and there was nowhere for him to sit. After he made the phone calls to cancel my plans for the day, I told him to go home, and that I would call him when I was done. After all, there was nothing he could do, and we had no privacy anyway.

After an x-ray to assess the damage, I was moved into the emergency area where there were a few beds, each with dividing curtains between them. By this time, the pain was under control. I was also warm and no longer shivering. The first words the kind doctor said to me were, "I'm sorry. I'm so very sorry." I was touched by his compassion. Then he told me that I had broken my ankle, the ligaments were badly torn, and that I needed surgery ASAP, followed by months of physiotherapy.

In that moment, the words reached my physical ears and I heard them. But I did not really hear them, because I did not digest any of that reality. I had never had surgery for a broken bone. I had never had physiotherapy, and to my knowledge, I had never seriously injured any ligaments. In some respects, it was all Greek to me.

As the doctor prepared to put a temporary cast on my foot, one which would require him to bend my ankle joint, that is, my newly displaced ankle joint, into a ninety degree angle, he told me that I wouldn't be walking for a while. He informed me that I also wouldn't be playing Pickleball again until the fall. The fall? That was well over nine months away! And yes, the bending of my ankle to put on the part plaster-part tensor cast hurt. A lot!

He sent me home with prescriptions for pain killers and anti inflammatories. I also had a surgery date in Guelph for Tuesday, December 3, 2019 at 2pm. The very next day.

I started that day thinking that it was just any other day, but it most certainly was not. That day was a day unlike any other, a one of a kind day, a day that would bring radical change into my life on so many levels, and my thinking for a lifetime. What I took for granted - walking, the freedom to go places, and a life with no physical pain - was no longer a reality. Everything had changed in an instant.

Isn't it amazing that while this event took place three years ago, I can still recall many of the details, emotions, and things that were said to me. I'm sure this is the same for anyone who has started what seemed to be a normal day only to find it to be one of the most challenging, life altering days. In my experience, remembering the details fades over time as the many lessons, blessings, and strange thankfulness replace the shock, trauma and negative experience.

In fact, I woke up on Wednesday, December 1, 2022 thinking it was my two year ankle break anniversary. To celebrate, I went skating, something I used to love to do prior to my accident. This is something that I now can do! As I read the words in this book once more, I realized the truth: my ankle break anniversary isn't December 1. It's December 2.

That means the trauma is and has been fading from my memory, and praise God for that. In its place, I now remember the amazing times of communion with the Lord, and the little blessings along the way. It's true.

In the moment, when our sudden suffering feels very fresh, we think that it will be permanently etched on our minds. Even so, I can now profess, that in time, with healing, and the Lord's friendship, the intensity of these traumatic events will fade as the new perspective, and things that God brings into our lives begins to be worked out.

For so long I never understood when people shared testimonies of how they were thankful for some of the worst things that had happened in their lives. But now, looking back, I'm in that place too. God met me on that cold arena floor and He continues to sustain me one day at a time as I look to Him, the founder and perfecter of my faith (see Hebrews 12:2).

He has no favourites. He can and will do the same for all who choose to cling to Him, trust in Him, and look for the good that does and will shine out of our own shattering experiences.

QUESTIONS:

1. Think about a time in your life that a day started off "normally" and became a day unlike any other because of trauma, pain, or suffering. In what way have you noticed that the intensity of the memories, emotions, and experience has lessened over time? If not, why do you think that is?

2. Where do you see God at work in Wendy's story? Thinking of your own life, and the difficulties you've experienced, recount where God was at work. Look at the little details that you might have previously considered "coincidences".

3. If you've experienced "sudden suffering" in the past, what's an example of good that came from that difficulty? What lessons did you learn at that time?

THREE

LIFE IS LIVED AFTER THE FACT

After leaving the hospital, and successfully using my rather weak arms to lift my body up and into Derek's truck - this took several tries and the advice of a passerby - we picked up the prescriptions at our local pharmacy.

Why I insisted on crutching my way through water and light snow to go into the pharmacy, and then crutch my way to the very back of the store, I have no idea. But that is what I did. Perhaps I wasn't thinking. Perhaps the drugs were working well. Or perhaps I was just a little bit stubborn! I'm not used to being dependent on anyone for physical things, or perhaps I am just stubborn?

As we waited for the prescriptions, Derek did some grocery shopping, something he would do many times over the next several months, and I began to call my family to tell them what had happened. I sat on the seat at the blood pressure machine stretching my newly casted leg out onto my crutches. I was only too happy to tell the pharmacists and anyone passing by what had happened to me. I called our sons, my parents, and my sisters to fill them in on the situation.

I didn't know then that I would become the subject of so many of my own conversations with people. I didn't know how much and how often I would talk about my experience. Nor did I know that my accident would become an event in my life - a pivot point - from which radical transformation would occur. I didn't know that my life would come to be measured before and after the accident. Interestingly, I have come to discover that we all talk about major events in our lives, both positive and negative, in "before and after" terms, such as:

before I was a believer in Christ; after I was born again

before we were married; after we were married

before we had children; after we had children

before our miscarriage; after our miscarriage

before the divorce; after the divorce

before he died; after he died

Insert your own situation. With every major event in life, so much of our thoughts and conversations are focused on the day the event occurred, for months, and even years following it. In the early days following painful or traumatic events, we long for things to go back to the way they were as if they never happened.

We don't want the event to be true or our lives to move forward. We want things to be normal again! However, the truth is that we do live forward, and we must live after the fact.

Derek and I went to a local restaurant for lunch after picking up my prescriptions. It was after noon by this time. We weren't entirely sure what to expect of the surgery, or of our lives for the next "while" other than life would look very different. Derek would have to do the apartment renovation alone, or with the help of Charles who would be home over his Christmas break from university. I would have to be a couch sitter for the better part of many weeks. In reality, it was months.

I really had no idea just how long it would be until I could resume somewhat normal activities, such as walking. Neither one of us was prepared for the disruptive change that had been foisted upon us. Then again, is anyone prepared for sudden, unexpected trials and difficulties that bring profound loss, grief, and life change?

From the time I got home around 1pm on the day of my accident, I lived on a four hour schedule for the next twenty four hours. That's because every four hours I could take a pill to help with the pain that had lessened, but could not be ignored. I also had to learn to use crutches and to practice using my arms to lift my body up from the sitting position. At times like these, you discover how strong or weak you are, and I soon found out that my arms were pretty wimpy.

I was in the waiting period before surgery. Surgery. December 3. The third day of the month. That's the point from which so much of my life would be measured, from when I would see the surgeon for check-ups, have conversations with physiotherapists, and even talk about, in my frustration, just how long my recovery was taking. It felt like forever at times!

I know it's the same for everyone who has experienced a sudden loss, illness, accident, shock, death, tragedy, or undergone major surgery. Life is measured from that day forward. It's as if the event and date has been stamped on our minds. It was so big that it caused a fundamental shift in us.

I know that my experience caused a seismic shift in me. I never ever thought that I would be a person who lived with physical pain and limitation. Up to that point, at fifty four years of age, I never had.

On Tuesday, December 3 at 11am, I headed to Guelph for the surgery. Derek drove me to the hospital for noon, got me registered and settled in, and then continued on to Kingston for a three day conference for work. My sister Liz had offered to take me home, and to care for me the first night after surgery. Charles had also volunteered to look after me until Derek got home. Amazingly, he had no classes that week since it was the end of the semester and his exams were scheduled to start in ten days. Also pretty amazing was the fact that the surgery was in Guelph, where Charles lived!

Around 12:30pm, I met the surgeon who explained that he was going to install a plate and screws in my ankle. The severity and seriousness of that did not register in my mind. The joke was that I would set off the airport security. That was pretty funny because I couldn't remember the last time I had even been in an airport, let alone needing to go through security.

Ironically since writing those words, I actually did have the opportunity to travel in October, 2021 when I accompanied a friend who was having back surgery in Germany. I did go through airport security several times, and ... I didn't set off the alarms! Too bad because I thought that would have been fun, but since my plate and screws are made of titanium, no alarms for me!

The surgeon told me that I would be coming back in two weeks and that I might be able to have a "boot cast". I got the impression from him - or I was desperately hoping - that it wouldn't be too long until I was walking, maybe six weeks. That sounded so good to me.

My surgery was set for 2pm, and as instructed, I had been fasting since midnight. Liz and Charles arrived not long after Derek left, and asked how I was doing. I was fine, pretty relaxed all things considered. I wasn't afraid as I had been through other surgeries, and I didn't know anyone who had experienced a surgery requiring plates or screws. I simply wasn't thinking much about it. Of course, I was on strong pain medication; my 10am pills were doing their job.

After a while, the doctor popped his head into my room to let me know there would be a slight delay. An hour went by, and I began to feel some pain. I asked the nurse if I could have something for pain as my 2pm pain pill time had passed. Her reply? "No. Not before surgery." Oh. More waiting. More delay. More pain.

Eventually, I told Liz and Charles to go shopping, that I would be fine, and that it wouldn't be long until I was in the operating room. At 3pm, I began to get a wee bit frustrated. I had been fasting since midnight, my stomach was growling, my foot was paining me, and my surgery wasn't happening!

Finally, at 4pm, the doctor came in and I was wheeled to the operating room. The halls were narrow, the eyes of the nurses and doctors were kind and compassionate, almost sad, but I didn't take note of that then. It has just hit me now. They definitely knew something that I wasn't aware of or chose not to comprehend. To be honest, I don't think anything registered before or after the surgery, where now for the first time in my life, I had "hardware".

I woke up from surgery with a partial cast, which consisted of plaster around my foot, and a tensor bandage around my leg, all the way up to my knee. The medication was not touching the pain, even though the recovery nurse was administering it every five minutes per the doctor's instructions.

It was now after 5pm. The surgeon had left for home and I still hadn't eaten all day! My recovery nurse called the surgeon on his cell phone to ask for advice on how to get my pain under control. This included changing the medication. Once the pain was managed, and I was fully awake, I was given instructions, both verbally and on paper:

"Take the painkillers every four hours as needed.
Elevate your foot.
Rest.
Do not bear any weight on your foot."

Liz and Charles returned to get me around 6pm. We grabbed a quick supper and Liz picked up my prescriptions. We arrived home around 8pm, and I went straight to bed.

Day one complete.

Who knew that it was from that day, that surgery day, that every day, week, month, and even years would be measured? My recovery would be measured from December 3, 2019. Not only did I need to recover physically, but I needed to recover emotionally, mentally and spiritually. It was as if my axis, perhaps even my foundation, had tilted. What I had expected of my life was no longer true. I had to come to grips with what had just happened, and what I actually believed about myself, about God, and about my life. And so will everyone who has had the rug pulled out, all their props removed, or if their worst nightmare has been realized.

One word of encouragement: life is worth living forward. Even though we measure from a moment in the past, there are good things coming for our future. It doesn't feel like it in the pain and fog, and it seems even insensitive to say it, but I know it to be true.

Today I thank God for what happened, because my life lived after my accident has shown me God's faithfulness, provision, love, and care, and it has exposed how much I needed to change my attitudes and expectations. I now have new hobbies, interests and a whole new theology on suffering and pain that I just wouldn't have had if my accident hadn't happened.

QUESTIONS:

1. Is there an event in your life that you continue to think upon from one certain date on the calendar? If so, what is it? How have you found yourself living a different kind of life than you did before? For example, do you have new hobbies, interests, or a whole new way of thinking?

2. Through your suffering experience, what thoughts, attitudes and expectations about your life, God, and others did you find needed changing?

3. What do you make of the statement, "...my accident would become an event in my life - a pivot point - from which radical transformation would occur?" In what ways have you experienced transformation in and following your seasons of suffering?

FOUR

DENIAL HAS A PURPOSE

"What did you say, Doctor?" Maybe it was the drugs. Maybe it was the pain. Maybe it was the shock. Maybe it was something else, but nothing the emergency doctor told me registered in my brain. His words gained no traction in my conscious thinking. I had no idea of the extent of damage to my ankle, or the drastic change that was coming into my life.

Perhaps it was just too much to process in that moment. The doctor said I wouldn't be walking as much as I used to, until the spring at the earliest, or playing Pickleball until maybe the fall. It was early December. I had just moved to Mt. Forest. I had just started playing this game. I was just meeting new people. I had a renovation of an apartment to do. The fall - that's nearly ten months away!

My thoughts were yelling, "This cannot be happening! No way! It can't be that bad, can it?" I'm not sure, but in that moment with the pain, the drugs, and perhaps my own disbelief, I simply refused to acknowledge the reality of my situation. After all, I broke my foot when I was a teenager, and it wasn't that bad. I remember it being no more than six weeks of the summer that I was out of commission. Here is my first journal entry:

Forced rest. Radical change in pace and lifestyle. Well Lord, I'm coming to you. Thank you for walking with me and I'm here, listening to what you have to say to me in these next few weeks.

(Journal, December 3, 2019)

Few weeks? Looking back, that is laughable. Just over a week later, I wrote:

Keep things in perspective. One leg. 6 weeks +. Not 6 months. Not a lifetime. Temporary.

(Journal, December 11, 2019)

I wrote "not 6 months", yet here I am at more than six months plus two years still experiencing the effects of my accident. After all, I do have "hardware" now where before I didn't.

Continuing on, ten days after my accident:

Wow. Not a great day. Feeling pain. I had some tears. I

just hear my Lord asking me to endure, to be patient, and to
persevere.

(Journal, December 12, 2019)

In those first few weeks, I wrote in my journal what I thought it meant to persevere and endure. I copied out the definitions of these words. I looked up and recorded many Scriptures about endurance. I listened to various sermons, and I just kept hearing the Holy Spirit talk to me about it. I wanted to have a good attitude through what I called my "trial". Even still, I don't think it fully registered. If the trial was going to be short - as I expected, or desperately hoped - why would I need to endure?

In the pain, the fog, the shock, and yes, the denial, I simply wasn't catching on to what was going on. At two weeks post surgery, it was time for a trip to Guelph to see my surgeon. Here's what I wrote before I went:

Thank you Lord for today, for providing for my needs. I
choose to trust you today whatever the result. I believe for a
good report – supercharged healing has occurred. Thank you for
strengthening my faith, my resolve, and my determination.
Thank you also for giving me limits. I will rest, wait, go slow,
and listen. I do truly believe that these 40 days (6 weeks) or
whatever time will have done its work.

(Journal, December 17, 2019)

The words in my journal illustrate how I was essentially telling the Lord how much time my healing would take. On the one hand, I said I would trust the Lord, while on the other, I twice declared that I would have a short recovery. My expectation was to be fully and completely healed with no more pain in my life, and in no more than six weeks. I thought that my life would be what it had been before the accident.

My life would be what it had been before the accident.

I had to write that sentence again because that is the epitome of denial. We want things to be as if they've never happened. Yet, that is denying that the thing really did happen! That's not the truth, and I'm convinced it isn't helpful. I believe that God can and does heal people fully, completely, and miraculously, but we are not promised this every time we experience trials or suffering. Jesus promised us tribulation (John 16:33).

There is good news, however, because we are also promised that Jesus is with us in these difficult times. David proclaimed, "Even though I walk through the valley of the shadow of death, I will fear no evil for you are with me" (Psalm 23:4a). There are times when we must walk through deep, dark, hard valleys, but we can rest assured and know, that the Lord is with us through it all, bringing comfort, if we allow Him to do so.

When we expect things to be as though nothing happened, it is good to keep this thought in mind: when Jesus appeared to Thomas after His death, burial, and resurrection, the evidence of his crucifixion was marked on His body. The holes in His hands and the gash in His side were there for Thomas to not only see but to touch (see John 20:24-28). Since Jesus Christ bears the marks of His physical suffering, why do we think that we won't?

The human condition is to want to avoid all pain and suffering. Yet, I have found that what God can do in and through sudden suffering is nothing short of miraculous, and it often occurs in our heart, mind and soul. However, this takes time.

It's a good idea to admit that things won't be the same. It doesn't mean they will be worse, but they will be different going forward. This thought, and these words are ones I had to remind myself of many times.

At my two week appointment, the partial cast was taken off, the bandage and staples were removed, and I was able to get a good look at my leg and ankle. What I saw wasn't pretty and it really surprised me. My leg and foot had shrunk. I had what looked like a long scar on the left side of my leg. That was where they had opened me up to install the plate. No wonder I often had pain in that area of my leg. At times, I actually couldn't figure out why that left side of my leg hurt so much!

I looked at my leg again to discover that my calf muscle,

or what had once been a calf muscle, had disappeared. My left leg was shaped totally differently than my right. The muscle had literally fallen. That was a real shock to me, and it saddened me. I really didn't expect that. My thought at seeing it was: "How much effort and work is it going to take to rebuild that muscle? It wasn't even much of a muscle anyway."

Interestingly, it was that very muscle that required the most physiotherapy help in the form of stretching, deep tissue massage, and laser therapy. Additionally, now three years later, I still find that my left calf muscle can be tighter than the right, so I continue to do stretches when needed.

I did get the boot cast at that appointment, which meant that I could take it off when sleeping. I could take showers, albeit sitting on a chair, and I could scratch the places that were itchy. If you've ever had a plaster cast, you'll know what I mean. Two firm foam pads were inserted under my heel as my foot couldn't bend fully in the walking position yet. Together the foam pads added up to an inch, which seems like a small amount, but it actually was quite significant. I was told that the boot might come off in four weeks, and that I might begin to bear some weight at that point.

That sounded fantastic. After all, bones heal after six weeks; everyone knows that, right? I was so pleased that my healing was coming along very well, thanks to God, the prayers of people, and my choice to keep resting. When the surgeon left, the nurse who had taken the staples out, turned to me and said, "That boot cast can't come off as long as the foam pads are there."

In my mind, I responded, "Ok. No problem! I will just make sure that the foam pads are gone by the time I come back at the six week mark." I figured I could do that!

I'm not sure when it was, but I started doing research into what had taken place. I didn't have a copy of the x-ray, and I wasn't bold enough to ask the surgeon to take a picture of it for me while it was up on the screen. However, I did recall the doctor using the term *O.R.I.F.* I had no idea what that even meant. Here is the explanation; please note the italics are for emphasis:

O.R.I.F. (Open Reduction Internal Fixation) is surgery to fix *severely* broken bones. It's only used for *serious* fractures that can't be treated with a cast or splint. These injuries are usually fractures that are *displaced*, *unstable* or those that involve the joint…'Open reduction' means a surgeon makes an incision to *re-align* the bone. 'Internal fixation' means the *bones are held together* with hardware like metal pins, plates, rods, or screws. After the bone heals, this hardware isn't removed. Generally, recovery takes *3 to 12 months*. Every surgery is different. Complete recovery depends on the type, severity and location of your fracture.[1]

Those key words I italicized? I sure wish I had done that at the time of reading it. Perhaps then I would have understood just how serious my situation was. All the time I kept thinking that my recovery would be short! I was declaring that God was going to supernaturally speed my healing. Looking back, I can see that I was telling God what I expected Him to do. As I read the description of my surgery today, I realize that my expectation of recovery was completely out of whack.

I would have needed nothing short of a miracle to heal in the time I was expecting. With God nothing is impossible, but God is also sovereign. He has a plan in our suffering, and He has a plan for our healing, that is, how long it takes, and the ways in which we will be healed.

We don't dictate what God should do. We yield to what He is doing, because we know that He is God, He is good, and He is always at work.

Fast forward to the time I had a physiotherapist coming to my home. On one particular day, early in his series of visits, he told me that I was making good progress. He also reminded me to keep up with the daily exercises. As I stood at the top of the stairs - all proud of myself - and he stood at the bottom, he turned to me just before he was about to leave.

This is what he said: "Ankles are tricky. Your foot won't feel normal for a year." My immediate thoughts were:
"What?"

"Noooooooooooooo."

I did not want to hear that. I was at six weeks when he said it, and it already felt like forever. So, I simply refused to believe what he said. After he left, I said out loud, "I refuse to accept that. I don't receive that." As a "faith-filled" Christian, I was taught to reject curses, and that was a curse. Or so I thought at the time. Let's not forget that God can and does turn curses into blessings. What may or may not have been a curse became a reality and a blessing in my life.

I believe that my reaction to the bad news I received indicates a classic case of denial. I can only say that looking back. If I had simply taken to heart what he had said, processed his words, and chosen to accept the understanding of this expert, I might have saved myself a lot of grief, frustration, disappointment, and discouragement.

Not only did this knowledgeable physiotherapist tell me it would take a year, but my internet search had said "three to twelve months". In addition, the emergency doctor had said I wouldn't be walking as much as I was used to, for a minimum of five months, or playing Pickleball for at least ten months. However, I didn't hear, process, or allow those facts to penetrate my mind. That length of time was just too long for me. The news was bad. While bones heal in six weeks, ligaments don't, and muscles take time to be re-built. That's the part I didn't grasp.

I can now hear in my story how I simply chose to deny

the truth that was right in front of me. Furthermore, I hadn't even talked to the Lord about what my physiotherapist said. I just rejected it outright. Yet, that man was telling me the truth because that's exactly what I experienced. I simply chose not to accept the severity of the situation.

According to the Kubler-Ross model, denial is the first stage of grief:

> Denial says 'this can't be happening to me.' Right after a loss, it can be hard to accept what happened. You may feel numb, have trouble believing that the loss really happened, or even deny the truth [2]

I didn't really understand that a huge part of what I was processing was grief. After all, I had lost my life as I knew it. I lost my mobility and freedom. I lost confidence in God and the pain free life I expected to live. These are all things I now see that I had not only taken for granted, but also felt entitled to have.

Yet, in an instant, my life was no longer the same. It was drastically and suddenly different. It most certainly was not what I expected. It was not what I hoped or wanted. I'm sure that is true for all people who have had to face a hardship that rocked their world to the very core. Mine was a broken ankle and physical pain, while already suffering grief and loss. It may not be like the experiences of others, but for me it was significant.

Denial isn't bad. It's the way we humans deal with shock and sudden change, loss, or trauma. It's not something to be ashamed of. I admit that I was in denial of my situation, even though I had many cold, hard facts in front of me. I wasn't facing the truth. I'm not sure how I would have responded had I fully understood just how much my life was going to change, and how alone I would feel. Any loss or difficulty in our lives is accompanied by grief. Listen to these words from the Apostle Peter: "In this you rejoice, though now for a little while, if necessary, you have been grieved by various trials" (1 Peter 1:6).

God knows that trials and difficulties will be met with strong emotions, including grief. I found the following quote on-line, and it does a good job of expressing grief and denial:

Grief is an overwhelming emotion. It's not unusual to respond to the intense and often sudden feelings by pretending the loss or change isn't happening. Denying it gives you time to more gradually absorb the news and begin to process it. This is a common defense mechanism and helps numb you to the intensity of the situation.[3]

Denial has a purpose. According to the quotes above, denying something "gives you time to more gradually absorb the news and begin to process it." I believe it is helpful for a time. However, it can become unhelpful, even unhealthy, if we stay in it. Stubborn refusal of reality does not help us move forward. Those closest to us can help in this since they can see things about us that we can't. They can lovingly confront us with the truth. There is a time when we must face reality and accept what has happened. It is essential to accept the truth, since it's the only way to move forward toward health, strength, wholeness, and yes, eventually joy.

QUESTIONS:

1. Describe a time in your life that you experienced the shock, denial, and grief Wendy talked about in her story.

2. What have you learned as you've moved from denial to reality? How did you finally get to the place of accepting the truth of your situation?

3. If you are currently in a state of denial in your life, would you say it has a purpose and is helping you? Or is it hindering you? Denial can be a problem when we choose to stay in it and not see the truth.

FIVE

"IT IS WHAT IT IS."

At four days in, on opiate drugs for pain, I was relegated to sitting on my couch every day with my leg raised up on another chair. I've never been one to sit a lot. I'm a do-er and a go-er, so this posture of sitting was new to me. What was also new was that my dear husband was now in full care-giver mode, a whole new posture for him. He brought me drinks, called me to the table for meals, which he had planned and cooked. He also played the card game "Skip Bo" with me most nights after he had cleaned up the kitchen. In addition, he ran to the store several times a week for groceries.

I had my crutches to get around. I traveled from the couch to the table, to the washroom, and to bed. I had my Bible and journal, several books to read, an adult colouring book and markers, my phone for contact with the outside world, and eventually my laptop. All these were placed around me.

Thankfully, I was able to stay on the main floor of our house for everything, including watching television, because for the first time in our married life, we had a TV in our bedroom! The only time I needed to use the stairs was to let our dog Sammy out into the backyard when Derek was at work during the day.

As I mentioned, it was only three days prior to my accident that Derek and I had taken ownership of an apartment building. Imagine the daunting weight of a full time job, a wife out of commission, and a huge renovation to get done so that the apartment could be rented. My husband had a lot on his plate, and on his mind.

On this fourth day of my recovery, I noticed that he wasn't overjoyed in any sense, and I knew I was the reason. Derek seemed tense and frustrated. He seemed impatient. Though it wasn't directed at me, I knew the situation we found ourselves in was the reason for his attitude.

When life hits a blow, it impacts everyone around us, especially the ones who love us the most. When our life has shifted drastically, so has theirs. Our loved ones do not like to see us hurting or sad, yet they feel helpless. They are not able to fix the situation or take away our pain.

The reality of any sudden suffering is that it couldn't have come at a worse time. The intensity of the emotions can be overwhelming for everyone connected to the situation. The truth is, if any of us chose a time to have a loss or difficulty, we'd likely say, "No thank you". However, life is such that these things do happen, and when they happen suddenly, we just have to go with it, ride it out, and accept it. We have to get out of denial eventually.

I had been reading verses in my Bible about enduring and persevering with a good attitude. Enduring. Persevering. As if that's not hard enough, I needed to have a good attitude? Upon noticing Derek's struggle, I felt I had to talk to him. At a minimum, I had to acknowledge his feelings in it all. I am a talker and a processor. I could have let it go. However, I knew, with this hard journey ahead of us, his attitudes and my responses were going to be critical for us both to endure and to be kind to one another.

I approached Derek and we talked about the situation, the very real inconvenience of it, and the reality that I would not be able to help with the apartment renovation. I couldn't help even when I could bear weight since the apartment was five floors up, with no elevator. I reminded him that we were both in this together, that I hadn't asked for it, caused it, or desired to be helpless, or even useless in a sense. I explained that we would have to learn a new normal for life. I also thanked him for everything he was doing, and out of my mouth popped this statement:

"It is what it is."

Isn't that the truth? When an awful, difficult, challenging thing happens, "It is what it is". We both had to accept that this was to be our new normal for a time. He was going to be my care giver and the one to shop for groceries, cook, clean, do laundry, as well as work at his job and renovate an apartment. It's what we had to accept, walk out, and work out together with love, patience, and grace for each other. "It is what it is" would be a line that Derek would need to remind me of on numerous occasions. In this little line are the beginnings of acceptance of the present reality of life. We live in the present realities of life. As denial is a coping mechanism, truly living in the now of life helps with not being hard on ourselves or others. This was going to be one of the greatest tests of our marriage and to my Type "A" personality, where things get done, and I'm the one who does them!

For the initial six weeks of "no weight bearing" and for many weeks beyond that, Derek would need to work at his job and renovate the apartment, leaving me alone for as many as eight to ten hours a day, six days a week.

"It is what it is."

Having just moved to the area, with no friends, and my family a couple of hours away, I didn't have people to rely on to help or support me.

"It is what it is."

Not being able to drive, walk, or go anywhere, I was now, for the first time since being a baby, dependent on others to take care of most of my basic needs.

"It is what it is."

In the end, these facts were exactly what I needed to draw closer to the Lord, to learn to rely on Him, AND to recognize that I was capable of doing some things, even in my weakened state.

"It is what it is."

Think about that line. It can and does help us to accept the reality of a challenging situation, and the best part of all is that God is right there with us. Though we wish we could turn back time, we can't. Instead, we can come to terms with what is currently happening in our lives, in this moment, and in this season of life. Here's my journal entry at nine weeks:

I sure don't like this pain, but it keeps driving me back to you, Lord.

(Journal, January 30, 2021)

"It is what it is" could be spoken and thought of with resignation, even bitterness, but focusing on or longing for what was, won't move us out of denial, or help to move us forward into what is. We really do need to get out of denial because the old has passed, and we are in the new. Granted, it's not a life we chose, but it is what it is.

This won't happen overnight. It's a process that takes time. We may need our loved ones to remind us of this many times. I have found that if we can come into some level of acceptance of what is, we can also consider the question: "Now what?" We can choose to accept what is, and move forward to what's next for us. In addition, we can begin to think about what we actually can do in the current situation.

I particularly like how Frank Viola encapsulated this in his book *Hang On, Let Go*:

"Let go of what's "supposed to be" and choose to accept what is for the present time." [4]

This is an idea I will expand on later in the book. The words "focus on what you can do, not on what you can't do" were words that I felt the Lord gently whispered in my heart at different times in my recovery journey. These words helped me immensely. There were things that I could do in my weakened state. There were ways I could stretch myself. Thinking about and doing those things led to a sense of purpose, and gave me moments of joy.

The Bible says that "God is our refuge and strength, a very present help in trouble" (Psalm 46:1). I can declare that through my "it is what it is" season, I saw and felt God's hand of favour, provision, and care many times. I pray that the pain, confusion, frustration, and "it is what it is" moments would be the very things that drives us back to God.

QUESTIONS:

1. In your suffering, if you reminded yourself of the statement, "It is what it is", how might it help you?

2. How have you seen your loved ones react and struggle when you are walking through suffering? Would "it is what it is" have helped them and you to move forward?

3. What situations in your life have driven you closer to God? Why do you think that is?

SIX

IT'S OKAY TO CRY

If you knew me, you would know that I cry....easily. I have cried during television commercials, movies, songs, while reading a greeting card, when praying, and when someone is telling me about his/her life. I can cry just as easily when I see someone else crying.

A friend once told me that my tear ducts are connected to my bladder, and it just might be true! I can cry at any little thing because I am someone who feels things deeply. Yet, with all the physical pain throughout the accident and emergency room experience, I don't remember crying once.

I believe the first tear fell immediately after we had picked up my pain medications. I put my newly casted left foot on the ground for a second when I lost my balance in a snow bank as I was trying to get into Derek's truck. I screamed out, and then cried a little.

Looking back, I wonder, "Was I just trying to be brave or had nothing really entered my conscious mind?" After all, I was on some pretty strong pain killers. I had been giggling in the ambulance and at the hospital too.

Eventually, the tears did fall. Life for me had radically changed. I couldn't walk. I couldn't do much of anything, and here I was in a community where I knew no one. Oh, how I had taken so much for granted!

When we move out of the denial stage, the emotions that have been hidden or suppressed will begin to rise. It's possible to be confronted with a lot of sorrow. This is a necessary part of the journey of grief, and it can be difficult. Emotions can be exaggerated and uncomfortable, and they can make themselves known at inopportune times. With every sudden life change or loss, grief is inevitable. When the shock fades and reality hits, grief follows. It should anyway, if we let it. No one likes unexpected change or loss.

At times when life doesn't seem fair, we could turn our grief into anger, and direct it at those around us, or at God. Alternatively, we could turn our grief inward, toward ourselves, which can result in depression. In our pain avoidance, we could numb, suppress, or continue to deny it, but trust me, that isn't healthy. It only delays the inevitable. The best alternative?

Turn to God and allow Him into the pain and sorrow.

One of the first times I remember feeling and expressing the deep sorrow at what I had lost was when I looked out the window one morning and saw a lady walking her dog. I burst into tears. I thought, "I can't walk my dog. I can't go walking. I can't enjoy the outdoors!" My reaction was very exaggerated. In that moment, I experienced a sense of acceptance, disappointment, and devastation at all that I had lost.

The title of this chapter came through a conversation I had with a friend after I told her that story. She said, "Wendy, it's okay to cry." That just struck a chord in me. For someone who is emotional, why did I need to hear that? It was as if I needed permission to go ahead and cry. I must have been trying to hold myself together, to be brave, and to be strong. Please don't do that! It's in our weakness that God is strong.

It's in our weakness that we allow human beings to enter into our pain with us. Grief, pain and sorrow need to be felt, expressed, and processed. This is the way forward.

The Bible says, "Blessed are those who mourn, for they shall be comforted" (Matthew 5:4). If we don't feel grief, we won't feel comfort. If we don't feel pain, we won't feel joy. If we don't allow our wounds to be open, we won't receive the healing that comes. The prophet Jeremiah said, "You can't heal a wound by saying it's not there!" (Jeremiah 6:14a, TLB).

So let's live in reality and admit life can hurt, and

sometimes it can be hard, really hard. We might as well work through the pain and the process, rather than stuff it down, deny it, or numb it. Here is a journal entry in a challenging moment:

Not a great night. I couldn't fall asleep. I fell on the floor in the middle of the night coming back from the bathroom, and I woke Derek up! I cried silently. Oh Lord, you knew all this would happen. This is such a maturing time – and the attitude I choose makes all the difference. I had a little cryfest today (ran over my foot with the wheelchair)– then I heard you say, "Don't quit. One day. One moment."

(Journal, December 14, 2019)

One day. One moment. Sometimes that's all we can focus on. When life shifts, everything in us has to adjust to a new way of doing things. The best advice I could give is this: don't quit. Keep going. Keep listening to the still small voice of God and the encouragement of the Holy Spirit.

The wonderful thing about being weak, about crying in our trouble, is that God is strong and He's our help and our comfort in these times. Tears are cleansing and healing. We need to let them out because bottled up they can do irreparable damage to us and others.

In the months of my recovery, there were countless other times and days that I cried and asked "Why did this happen?" There were many days that I felt sorry for myself. At times, I would sit and cry, sometimes in the presence of my husband, and sometimes alone. Let the tears flow! It's actually healthy, it's helpful, and it allows us to feel the pain, and receive comfort from God as we cry out to Him. The entries below illustrate other challenging days I had:

Shoe doesn't fit well today. That got me so frustrated. I complained and I cried.

(Journal January 20, 2020)

The physical pain is intense today. I have had to take two doses of Extra Strength Tylenol. In tears. I can hardly take it – this journey is hard – so very hard. I'm so not used to pain.

(Journal March 1, 2020)

Pain is an important part of the human condition, since without it, we wouldn't avoid dangerous situations, slow down, or get things checked out. Pain is the body's warning system, and it needs to be attended to - not just physical pain, but emotional pain as well. It screams and won't be ignored.

Pushing it down, numbing it with drugs, alcohol, social media, Netflix binges, or podcasts doesn't work. It might provide temporary relief in the moment, but over time, it is no way to deal with pain and the reality of life. It will not help us to move forward, and it might actually cause us to get stuck.

How many of us have grown up believing that tears are weakness, that we are to put on a brave face and a stiff upper lip, and all that? I think many of us have also been told that somehow to cry or lament indicates a lack of faith.

I am convinced that our acceptance of what is true is crucial to moving forward. Living in denial only delays the inevitable and that isn't helpful. Later in the book, I talk about how it's not helpful to our recovery or our faith to get stuck in a pity party. When we live in the truth of our situation, and in who God is and what He says, we can come into a place of acceptance, thanksgiving, and joy in the middle of our difficulty.

The Psalmist said, "Weeping may tarry for the night, but joy comes with the morning" (Psalm 30:5b). I didn't feel or believe those words at the start of my sudden suffering, however, over time, I have found them to be very true. My time of suffering was a time of tremendous growth, transformation and dependence on Christ. My sorrow eventually led to joy when I saw what God had done for me. I saw His hand of provision in so many ways that it left me in awe and wonder.

The Lord carries us as we walk through the valleys and deserts of life, but we have to choose to stay connected, talking to Him and yes, crying through it all if necessary.

QUESTIONS:

1. In your struggles, pain, and suffering, have you allowed the reality and grief of your situation to hit you? Have you expressed your emotions? If not, why do you think that is?

2. Have you ever numbed or pushed down the strong emotions you feel at times? How has that impacted your life?

3. Why do you think our society promotes the "suck it up", "stiff upper lip" mentality when that doesn't help us to heal properly?

SEVEN

GOD IS UP TO SOMETHING

Consider it wholly joyful, my brethren, whenever you are enveloped in or encounter trials of any sort or fall into various temptations. Be assured and understand that the trial and proving of your faith bring out endurance and steadfastness and patience. But let endurance and steadfastness and patience have full play and do a thorough work, so that you may be [people] perfectly and fully developed [with no defects], lacking in nothing. (James 1:2-4, AMPC)

These words in the book of James are definitely not the words we want to hear when we encounter difficulties in life, but we need to hear them. In the moments, days, weeks, and potentially months following a sudden difficulty, our flesh screams for relief. Our hearts want justice. Our soul wants sympathy. We ask questions like:

"Why God?"
"Why did this happen to me?", and
"What did I do to deserve this?"

Please know that those are questions we all ask and God can handle them, but it won't be long until we discover that those questions often don't come with answers. Please don't listen to any human beings in your life who attempt to give an easy or simple answer to the hard questions you are asking. There are no easy or simple explanations to life's most difficult questions. Sometimes it's necessary to simply sit without the answers for awhile to allow God to reveal Himself.

One of the ladies in the Bible study group we had just started attending commented in the following way, after I told her about my accident: "I wonder what God is up to?" At the time I didn't like that thought.

My question was, "Why did this happen? Here I am trying to exercise and make new friends. I'm an empty nester for the first time, living in a new community, with a husband who is away at work all day, and we have a major renovation to do on an apartment building we just bought." I wonder what God is up to?

To be honest, I didn't wonder what God was up to in the early days and weeks of my recovery. I was in shock, confusion, denial, grief, and yes, a fair amount of self pity.

John Eldredge wrote a book titled *The Sacred Romance.* In it, he mentions that he shared with his friend Brent the details of a painful betrayal. Brent responded by saying, "I wonder what God is up to in all of this?" There's that question again! Here's John's response:

'God? What's he got to do with it?' My practical agnosticism was revealed. I was caught up in the social drama of the smaller story, completely blind to the true story at that point in my life. Brent's question arrested my attention and brought it to a higher level. In fact, the process of our sanctification, our journey rests entirely on our ability to see life from the basis of that question. [5]

What an insight! It bears repeating: "The process of our sanctification, our journey rests entirely on our ability to see life from the basis of that question."

I wonder what God is up to in all of this?

I did eventually get to the point in my recovery that I asked that question, but it took time. It's important not to rush. We've got to feel our feelings, ask the hard questions, and let God reveal Himself in His time, in His unique and personal way. For me, I did begin to see that He was up to something.

He was up to refining my thinking and my expectations of what life as a Christian looks like. He used that particular trial to stretch my faith in ways it had never been stretched before. When a trainer is building muscle, they literally have to exert and shred the muscles. As the muscles heal, they get stronger.

Our faith muscles are exercised more in times of trouble than in times of plenty. I'm convinced now more than ever that it takes more faith to endure a long recovery, than it does to receive instant healing.

Early in my recovery, I felt the Lord asking me to endure, and I did want to persevere with a good attitude. This Scripture in James really speaks to the need for endurance, steadfastness and patience in trials. Looking back, I realize that I was expecting, even telling the Lord how short my trial would be.

That's the funny thing: trials don't work that way. We don't get to decide how long or how short they will be. There's a work that God is doing in us, and the fact remains: trials take as long as they take. We don't know the work God will do, is doing, or what He wants to do in us through our trials.

Why? Because God has a purpose in each and every one of them, and at the time He may not let us know what He's up to. After all, He is God. Revelation and understanding come in time.

Endurance and patience may not be required in short trials, but they are absolutely required in long ones. Looking back, I can see now that in my immobility and separation from everything that was familiar, I was captive to all that God wanted to say to me and do in me.

I needed a major reconstruction in some of my core beliefs about God, myself, and my life. God knew what He was doing when He allowed me to be forced into a hidden and alone place for many months.

Maintaining connection with God when we are angry or disappointed is vital. It's natural to want to blame someone. When there's an accident or what seems like a fluke of nature, we want to blame God. But blame can stir up bitterness, lead to a victim mentality, and turn our hearts away from the Lord, when we need Him more than anything in times of trouble. Scripture says,

When you pass through the waters, I will be with you; and through the rivers, they shall not overwhelm you; when you walk through fire, you shall not be burned, and the flame shall not consume you. (Isaiah 43:2).

These are encouraging words in times of deep trouble, times of confusion, grief, suffering, and loss. While I was trying to sort out why I had such a destructive break in such a lonely time of my life, I made a conscious choice to bring God in, instead of pushing Him away. Here's what I mean:

Last night was yet another breaking point. Pain. Frustration. Tears. And a declaration of trust in my Lord.
(Journal, December 27, 2019)

In the middle of our pain, frustration, tears, sorrow, and angst, we can declare our trust in God. These things can co-exist. Trust and frustration. Lamenting is not a sign of a lack of trust. It's a sign of being human and not understanding life at times. After all, we aren't God and we don't know all things. Staying in touch with our emotions is a good thing. It's how we heal, and it's how we will be able to have compassion for others who go through similar things.

Draw near to God. Don't draw back or avoid Him, and definitely do not avoid the negative feelings. It is good to feel them, express them, and to talk to God about them. Even if we don't feel His presence, the truth is that He is with us. He is close to the broken hearted. These are truths to hang onto.

These are truths that can and must be rehearsed, declared, and remembered in dark times. Our flesh rises up, but when we practice truth, we are calmed. Here's another journal entry, just over a month after my accident:

I feel like I'm grieving some more — not sure what's going on. Father, I thank you for teaching me how to endure and be

patient. Every day I need to choose your way, your attitude, your heart. Honestly, this is really hard. Really frustrating. Sometimes so boring. And yet I know this is where you have me – in the palm of your hands – for a season, for a purpose.
(Journal, January 8, 2020)

I encourage you to bring God in. Don't push Him away. Truly, there is a friend who sticks closer than a brother (Proverbs 18:24). The Holy Spirit really does become a close friend when our world is spinning off its axis because of the sudden change that's been foisted upon us, and when our hearts are reeling.

There is a still small voice who will hush the chaos whirling around our emotions. He is with us, and He is at work. People can't understand and often don't have God's perspective, but He is always up to something, and He will reveal Himself in time.

QUESTIONS:

1. How might the question, "God, what are you up to?" help you in a current difficult situation you face, or how might it have helped you in the past?

2. Are you rehearsing the truth that the Lord is with you, even when you don't feel His presence? Are you turning to Him, and drawing close to Him even in your pain, grief, suffering, confusion and shock? If so, are you also experiencing His peace and presence?

3. What are some practical steps that will bring you closer to God?

EIGHT

CRY OUT TO GOD

The book of Psalms is full of lament and it is full of praise. Here are two examples:

> "On the day I called, you answered me;
> my strength of soul you increased."
> (Psalm 138:3)

> "In my distress, I called to the Lord, and he answered me."
> (Psalm 120:1)

It's good to lament and it's good to praise. We are emotional beings and feeling things deeply is healthy. Bottling up our emotions or pushing them down is unhealthy; as is pretending they aren't there. We shouldn't shy away from expressing our pain and sorrow, but it helps to turn our prayers towards the Lord. After all, He is a very present help in times of trouble. I wrote this in my journal, to encourage myself:

God is teaching me to grow up – to mature – big girl pants. Persevere. Continue. Don't give up. His strength is available. I can access it when I call on His name.

(Journal December 14, 2019)

We can be sure that when we cry out to God, He hears us and He will answer. It may not be in the way we hope or expect, but He will answer. Many times in my recovery journey I cried out to God. I knew that He not only heard me, but He answered.

So much of our faith journey during trials is choosing to believe that God is who He says He is, and that the words in the Bible are true. Even when the pain didn't go away, when the trial didn't end, and when nothing in my circumstances had changed, after crying out to the Lord, I had a measure of peace. I had hope. I knew that God was with me. He had not forsaken me.

In my lonely and alone times working through the recovery of my sudden suffering, as well as in other seasons of brokenness, I have found that God's voice can become quite loud. His presence can feel very near. I have heard His love and encouragement for me more clearly in my broken times than at other times in my life!

I have known that He was listening, and He has calmed me. My situation may not have changed - I may still be suffering and in pain - but my emotions can change. Joy can and does rise up from within, even in the middle of hardship.

There will be times we feel alone or think that no one understands. The truth is that people can't understand fully what we are experiencing unless they've experienced it also. But God does understand. There's no human being who suffered more betrayal, loss, rejection, or physical pain than our Lord Jesus Christ. He understands the deep pain we feel at times, and He is the one who promised to be with us and to never leave us. To be in Christ is to never be alone. We have the Holy Spirit in us, and Jesus is with us.

At more than a year post surgery, I experienced some nasty pain in my left ankle. I was in agony, not only physically, but emotionally as well. On one particular day, I sat in what felt like an ash heap and cried because I couldn't understand why, after all this time, I still wasn't fully healed. When I say an "ash heap", I am referring to the ancient practice in biblical times when people would mourn by wearing sack cloth and ashes. They would cover themselves in ashes as a sign of their grief.

During the time of my recurring pain, I was doing a Bible study, and I was directed to the passage in 1 Samuel 2 - "Hannah's prayer". The account of her story is in 1 Samuel 1:1-2:10. The revelation I had was that when

Hannah cried out to the Lord in the middle of her intense sorrow and suffering, her resultant emotions were peace, calm, and joy. Nothing in her circumstances had changed, yet following her lament, she felt relief, she experienced God, and she was able to move forward with her life. This was profound to me at the time I read it.

After reading Hannah's prayer several times in many different versions of the Bible, I too began to cry out to the Lord. Like Hannah, I experienced a deep sense of calm, peace, and joy after lamenting. I had the peace of God even though nothing else had changed. I felt His presence and care for me.

It was from that day on that I knew what I had to do: go back to physiotherapy. It had been many months since I'd been in physiotherapy, but I couldn't suffer through the pain without external help. I had talked to my doctor's office about getting pain medications, but they said no. I don't know why the pain reared its ugly head again, but it did. After a course of physiotherapy and a new revelation about the shepherd heart of God, I did get relief from the intensity of the pain.

Through my trial, I learned that I had to get quiet enough to hear God's voice of comfort. I had to feel the deep sense of loss in order to feel His nearness. Numbing and drowning pain, sorrow, anger, or other difficult feelings isn't the answer. We will only tune out the very One we need to tune into. That's why I strongly implore anyone who is suffering: do not drown out the emotions and thoughts with television shows, music, social media, Netflix, or other time-wasting activities. I chose not to spend much time listening to worship music or Christian podcasts either. That's not what was needed.

Here is what is needed at times of distress and trial: getting quiet, talking to the One who holds us and who is close to us, who wants more than anything to quiet us so that we can hear Him.

Think on these words of truth, "The LORD your God is in your midst, a mighty one who will save; he will rejoice over you with gladness; he will quiet you by His love; he will exult over you with loud singing" (Zephaniah 3:17). That is the character of God in the middle of our pain and suffering.

QUESTIONS:

1. What do you think of the contrast between lamenting through pain and suffering, while at the same time praising the Lord for who He is?

2. Have you experienced the peace and presence of the Lord following a time of crying out to Him? Were you able to get quiet enough to hear Him?

3. If you've never cried out to God in the middle of deep pain, loneliness, grief, or suffering, why do you think that is?

NINE

GIVING THANKS TAKES US HIGHER

Day after day after day, while I sat on the love seat in my living room with my foot up on a chair, wearing my pyjamas and bathrobe, I couldn't help but notice a sign on our wall that read:

"Begin each day with a grateful heart."

Some days, that sign was an annoying reminder, but I needed it. It's so easy to take the path of complaining and whining when things don't go the way we thought or expected they would. There is something wonderful about offering a sacrifice of praise in the middle of storms, trials, and difficulties (see Hebrews 13:15).

I've known quite a few people who have very little in life materially speaking, even ones who have lived on the street for a time, and they say, "There is always one thing to be thankful for". Whatever situation, season, or circumstance we find ourselves in, what is one thing we can be thankful for? I know if we really think about it, there's far more than just one.

The Apostle Paul said, "Rejoice always, pray without ceasing, give thanks in all circumstances; for this is the will of God in Christ Jesus for you" (1 Thessalonians 5:16-18). He didn't say, be thankful for the circumstance, but rather be thankful in the circumstance. This was the man who was in jail when he wrote those words. This was the man who was tortured, stoned, beaten, shipwrecked, and in danger from all kinds of people who were out to kill him. He demonstrates how he learned to be content, with little and with plenty.

I was coming to terms with having an attitude of gratitude when I wrote the following words in my journal:

We can choose our attitude when life throws a curve ball. I must choose joy, gratitude, and peace. The alternative is sadness, depression, and frustration – and they don't change a thing.
(Journal, December 31, 2019)

Learning comes through practice, through repeated behaviour; and all behaviour begins in our minds, with our thoughts. Though not easy, we can intentionally turn our thoughts to things that are lovely, worthy of praise, and honourable (Philippians 4:8). We can take every thought captive to obey Christ (2 Corinthians 10:5). Is this easy? No! But it is possible. It's a choice; a good choice.

Staying on the negative record of blame, anger, whining and complaining gets us nowhere fast. That line of thinking can be compared to what hamsters do on a wheel - they run around and around but they don't actually go anywhere. It is what kept the Israelites in the wilderness for forty years!

Choosing to draw near to God, to cry out to Him, to raise our eyes above ourselves - these things will help bring us out of the dark pit of sadness, hopelessness, or despair, and will render many blessings in the journey. We can all learn to be content, to enjoy the little things, and to be thankful regardless of the circumstance we find ourselves in. It really is possible to be thankful in any situation if we look beyond ourselves, if we but pay attention to what's around us.

Suddenly the things I was taking for granted became huge blessings for me. I wrote these words:

I praise you today because you are good. You are faithful. I trust you today and I surrender. I want to grow, change, and learn in this season. There's always something to be gained in every season – fellowship with you dear Lord is the best benefit. Quiet moments in your presence. I thank you for looking after all the details at the apartment building. Thank you for my

*dear husband who is looking after me so well, and for our sweet
dog who is by my side.*

(Journal, December 9, 2019)

With a little prompt from the sign on the wall, I could
choose thankfulness in the middle of my difficulty. This can
be done when we look at what and who we have around
us. I had a warm house, a couch to sit on, and a dog by my
side. I had eyes to see out the window, food in the fridge,
and a Bible to read. I had a relationship with the Lord, so
I could always talk to Him.

At that point, we had rented a wheelchair, so I was
able to get around, make myself a coffee, pour a water, do
the dishes, clear the dishwasher, and make a light meal.
These things were very exciting at the time! In fact, one day
when I cleaned the sink until it sparkled, I celebrated and
rejoiced. Strange, but true. For me, it was such a blessing to
once again be able to do something, something that made
my surroundings nicer.

I think it's absolutely crucial in recovery and healing no
matter what we are going through, to practice thankfulness.
But don't take my word for it. There is all kinds of research
in this field. Here's just one quote I found:

Gratitude reduces a multitude of toxic emotions, ranging
from envy and resentment to frustration and regret. Robert A.
Emmons, Ph.D., a leading gratitude researcher, has conducted

multiple studies on the link between gratitude and well-being. His research confirms that gratitude effectively increases happiness and reduces depression. [6]

A leading neuroscientist, Dr Caroline Leaf says:

Gratitude is a free 'antidepressant': When we express gratitude and receive the same, our brain releases dopamine and serotonin, the two crucial neurotransmitters responsible for our emotions, and they make us feel 'good'. They enhance our mood immediately, making us feel happy from the inside. Counting Blessings vs Burdens (2003), a study conducted on evaluating the effect of gratitude on physical well-being, indicated that 16% of the patients who kept a gratitude journal reported reduced pain symptoms and were more willing to work out and cooperate with the treatment procedure. A deeper dig into the cause unleashed that by regulating the level of dopamine, gratitude fills us with more vitality, thereby reducing subjective feelings of pain.

McCraty and colleagues (1998), in one of their studies on gratitude and appreciation found that participants who felt grateful showed a marked reduction in the level of cortisol, the stress hormone. They had better cardiac functioning and were more resilient to emotional setbacks and negative experiences. [7]

I have found that writing down what I'm thankful for is a good practice. So is thanking the people around me for what they are doing or have done. True appreciation is part of thankfulness. I am convinced that thankfulness takes us higher - gets our minds, thoughts, and emotions off of ourselves and onto God. Thankfulness has us thinking about things outside of ourselves. There is always one thing to be thankful for in every circumstance, and the benefits of having an attitude of gratitude are many.

QUESTIONS:

1. What are you thankful for at this time and season of your life, whether it be a time of plenty or a time of lack, a time of ease, or a time of significant difficulty?

2. How would you explain the statement "giving thanks takes us higher"?

3. In what ways do you practice gratitude?

TEN

SAY GOODBYE TO PRIDE

Pride grows in most soils, most climates. There are few
conditions under which it can't survive, even thrive. But
there is one soil that usually withers pride. It's brokenness. [8]

I have found the statement above by Mark Buchanan to
be true and it is something I have learned first hand. When
loss, pain, sickness, and sudden difficulty puts us in a place
of vulnerability, it becomes very apparent that we can't do
life on our own. We don't have it all together all the time,
and we actually do need help from others. It's not an easy
place to be, but it's a good place to be. In this self-sufficient,
stiff upper lip culture we live in, this is hard. To admit
weakness, brokenness, and dependence isn't something that
comes easily for most of us, but it is a posture that offers
tremendous blessings, from God and from people.

The day after my surgery, a young lady from the Bible study group we had been attending, brought us supper. One of the ladies from Pickleball brought a poinsettia, and my neighbour brought muffins and visited with me. Over the next few weeks, other people from the church and PickleBall, many who didn't know us, brought a meal or offered to sit and chat with me. Several friends from Owen Sound also made the trip; a few came more than once! They brought a meal, books to read, or gifts to enjoy; all came to spend time with me. I so appreciated this!

Often, it felt like oxygen to my soul to have someone sit in the same room with me, to talk, laugh, and pray together. To know that someone cared touched me deeply. I had never really been on the receiving end of these kinds of gestures because I had never been in a place of such vulnerability and weakness before. I probably came across as strong, and I might have even turned down offers of help in the past. I see now - that is pride at work. It really was a good kind of humbling to receive love from others.

These kindnesses helped me to accept that I was not alone in my suffering, even though at times I felt alone. Furthermore, I came to understand, that those people felt blessed to be able to help in some way. So often we don't know what to do or how to help a person who is suffering. But trust me, to say yes to anything that is offered is good for us when we are in a weakened or broken state, and it's good for the ones offering the help.

The first two weeks post surgery, I had a cast on my leg and was instructed not to get it wet. I couldn't bear weight on my foot either, so the idea of showers or baths was out of the question. In the first week of this, a new acquaintance came for coffee. I was in my pyjamas. This was and is not my usual attire when visitors come, but it's all I could wear because my regular pants wouldn't go over the cast.

Goodbye pride!

I told her how long it had been since I'd washed my hair, let alone had a shower! I could clean myself, sponge bath style, while sitting on a chair, but washing my hair seemed far more difficult. Her response was to simply offer to come and wash my hair for me. To let someone wash your greasy hair is a very intimate thing. Had my sister or a close friend offered, I would have said "yes", but this was someone I didn't know well. This was a place of true vulnerability for me.

What a blessing it was to say "yes", and to allow her to minister to me in this way. It meant another visit, another coffee, and squeaky clean hair.

Saying goodbye to pride and "yes" to help from others results in blessings, encouragement, and felt love. I highly recommend it!

In the same way, it is sometimes necessary for us to

humble ourselves and ask for help.

Goodbye pride!

I had to ask Derek and Charles for glasses of water, cups of coffee, or things from downstairs that I wanted to have around me on my couch, which I later called my "command centre". This was usually daily, and sometimes several times a day! At the start of my recovery, it just took too much out of me to have to bum it up and down the stairs to retrieve the things I needed/wanted from my office in the basement. With crutches, I only had my two hands to crutch with, so I couldn't carry a drink.

With Christmas around the corner, and no shopping completed, I had to reach out to people to ask them to buy gifts for me to give to my family. They always said, "yes". I'm not used to asking for help, so it was quite humbling.

Goodbye pride!

I didn't want to put anyone out, but maybe I needed to exercise my vulnerability muscle. Each and every person expressed his or her willingness and joy in being able to help, and when the item was brought to me, we often had a visit together.

On a whim, I called the local VON to see if they could come to do light cleaning or to help me get in and out of the shower when Derek was away at work, and Charles was back at university. This was assuming I would get my boot cast of course. I was a little nervous about being alone and possibly slipping while getting in or out of the shower. By God's grace, they had an opening for me at the end of December, and I did get my boot cast mid-December.

Again, it was humbling to allow someone into my house while I sat in my pyjamas, with he house getting dirtier every day. I had practiced putting the chair in the shower, getting on the chair, taking a shower, and getting off the chair while bearing no weight on my left foot! These were huge steps of progress for me at the time. Thankfully, I managed to do this each time the PSW came, and I didn't have to completely bare myself to her!

She came once a week for an hour a day. Her company was nice - someone to talk to - and so was having help in the mundane things that had to get done, like vacuuming, cleaning bathrooms, washing dishes, and eventually putting away all of the Christmas decorations. Every time she visited, she reminded me that, "slow and steady is best". She also warned me that I might have a set-back from time to time. This was something I didn't want to hear, but I needed her wisdom.

She was a great advocate too; she arranged for me to have in-home physiotherapy. I couldn't walk, it was winter, and I couldn't get down what seemed to be a giant step from my front door to the driveway. I didn't know many people who had the time to give me rides to and from physiotherapy during the day. This was another time I needed to remember: "It is what it is".

When the in-home physiotherapist came, he taught me range of motion, stretching and strengthening exercises, and helped me to bear weight on my foot. It was with this man that I took my first steps again while he held my hands. He was the one who told me, "It will take about a year for your foot to feel normal".

As I said earlier, I simply shut my ears to that possibility. I declared supernatural healing over my ankle and desperately wanted to have that be my reality. I didn't want to be in a place of pain or vulnerability for a year or more.

The most powerful pride killer was when I realized I had an expectation of being completely set free from all pain. I expected no residual effects of any kind after I was healed! I was convinced that I wouldn't have to go through this "trial" for long. I was so desperate for the pain to be over that I talked myself into believing that God would give me a miracle. On February 1st, my 55th birthday, with cane in hand, and now bearing weight, a friend took me to a conference in Toronto. The focus was on healing. I had prayed prior to this, telling God I'd accept His will whatever it was, but secretly hoping to get called out from the crowd to come forward for prayer. Afterwards, I thought, I'd be jumping and running around like the man at the Beautiful gate in the Bible (see Acts 3:1-9).

Well, it didn't happen. I wasn't called out. I didn't jump and run around. I was prayed over many times by people sitting near me, but nothing else happened. There was no difference. No change. I think part of the reason I really wanted this instant healing was to be able to walk into our church on Sunday with my miracle so that God could be glorified, and these dear folks would see proof of miraculous healing.

I cringe as I write that because it sounds really awful, prideful and more about me than about God. I was somewhat disappointed when it didn't happen, but again I submitted myself to the Lord. My pride had to be stomped on through the process of walking again, and having to put my leg up during worship because I couldn't stand long.

I had to say "no" to activities and people, admit my limitations, and learn to live one day at a time. Accept limitations? That was perhaps one of the greatest pride crushers I experienced. These were difficult and extraordinarily useful times for me to learn to appreciate people and to take baby steps of progress.

I had to have a second surgery a year after the first one. This was to remove a troublesome ganglion cyst that pressed on my nerves and caused pain every time I walked, which prolonged my overall recovery.

Then about eight months after that, I experienced intense pain when walking. I bought a new pair of running shoes, thinking I just needed some extra arch support. But one day, the pain was so bad, I called my surgeon's office on the verge of tears. I left a message for the receptionist, telling her that I wanted to have the hardware removed because it was causing me pain. I was practically despairing that day. I was so sick and tired of having to deal with pain and an ankle that wasn't "normal".

It turns out that I had developed plantar fasciitis, and if you've ever had it, you will know what I am talking about. This led to four more sessions of a different kind of physiotherapy, learning new stretching exercises, and being reminded to do my daily physiotherapy exercises from the first surgery. I am still working this out, and I continue to learn to accept limitations.

Now I need to wear shoes indoors, and I can no longer walk barefoot without experiencing pain in the arch of my left foot - the one that I broke! I need to learn to pace myself with physical activities, and take time to rest my left foot if I am doing a lot. I need to continue to practice being kind to myself, and not pushing myself to the point of pain.

These are on-going lessons I had seriously hoped I didn't have to go through. I had always hoped and prayed, and believed that I wouldn't experience any lasting effects from my broken ankle and resulting surgery. But I do. I continue to say goodbye to pride, and learn to be dependent on the Lord, and not so self sufficient or entitled about my physical health.

I suppose I had need of some serious pride crushing to get to the place of understanding that I'm not God. I'm not in control of all things, or anything, and that He is.

Perhaps I had to see just how much pride I had in my life and what a sense of entitlement I had. Each of us has some level of pride operating in our lives. Rather than resist the process of these crushings and the need for vulnerability, remember this: God is strong when we are weak, and there are people around us who would love to help us in our weakness. It's a really beautiful thing to feel the love of people who care. It's just so worth it to accept offered help and to ask for help at times. In fact, it's part of the sense of blessing we experience through our hardship and difficulty.

QUESTIONS:

1. Where do you see pride at work in your life, and especially in times when you've had sudden suffering, grief, or weakness?

2. Are you someone who is willing to ask or accept help? Or are you more likely to want to appear strong and put together?

3. When you've helped others in their times of vulnerability, how have you found it to be a blessing for you as well as for the other person? Recount a time in your life that this was true for you.

ELEVEN

HOLD ONTO GOD'S WORD

On January 21, 2020, I joined a Ladies Bible study on First Peter. The leader, the same woman who washed my hair for me, offered to pick me up. To be honest, I hesitated at saying yes, because I knew just what a rigamarole it would be to get me to and from the church. She was only too willing to help so that I could take part in the Bible study. At the time, I didn't know just how much I needed to be there, or how much the words from this particular book of the Bible would minister to me.

Each week of the study included reading all of First Peter, completing homework questions, meeting together to share what we were learning, watching a video, and praying for each other. I recall the Lord urging me to share vulnerably about my life and the circumstance I was currently facing, as this would encourage others to get real with the struggles they too were experiencing. It was an eight week study, and four weeks into it, I wrote this in my journal:

Lord, is there anything you need me to know – following the study? Anything I'm missing in submission? I feel like you've already shown me so much. But Lord, I'm willing to go deeper and lower if that's what you require of me.

(Journal, February 18, 2020)

Then I recorded this verse:

And after you have suffered a little while, the God of all grace who has called you to his eternal glory in Christ, will Himself perfect, confirm, strengthen and establish you. (1 Peter 5:10, NASB)

Something about those words really struck a chord in me. It was if there were neon lights pointing to it with a sign saying, "pay attention to this!" I don't think I fully understood what I was choosing to submit to: the process of my recovery and how long it would feel, let alone how long it would take. The Apostle Peter didn't indicate any time length either. He simply said, "after you have suffered a little while".

To be honest, I wanted my "little while" to be a whole lot shorter than it was, but I have come to realize that some people suffer all their lives, and that's still "a little while" in light of eternity.

I studied, meditated on, and memorized First Peter 5:10 for the remainder of our study. I held onto it every day. I took it as a promise for me. I believed that I was only going to suffer "a little while", and then God Himself would "perfect, confirm, strengthen and establish" me, literally, that is, in my physical body.

Granted, Peter was not specifically speaking to his listeners about my situation. These words were an encouragement and exhortation in the face of what these Jewish followers of Christ were facing. Not only had they been displaced from their homes and mistreated by the Romans under Emperor Nero, they were also being severely persecuted by the Jews who were not following Jesus Christ.

This was a very different situation from mine. Yet, I believe that the Word of God is living and active, and that the Lord can and does speak through His Word into our circumstances. On February 24, 2020 I read that verse in various versions of the Bible. I spoke it out loud, wrote it down, and declared it to be the truth for my situation. I earnestly wanted it to be my reality.

I began to proclaim that I would experience complete restoration and strengthening in my left foot, so much so, that it would be as if it never happened. God can do that. He does do that today. However, He doesn't always do that.

While there's nothing wrong with declaring promises

in the Bible, sometimes we make assumptions. I know now that I was declaring those words from a place of expectation, again from that sense of entitlement, that my life would not and could not be marked with on-going suffering or limitation. I think it was more my flesh than my faith talking.

Looking back, I can see that I wasn't making room to hear what God might be wanting to say to me through the Scriptures. I simply knew what I wanted and expected.

I'd like to share with you how I studied and interpreted the Scriptures in the time of my recovery, and how a year later, God re-arranged my thinking. He dramatically changed the way I viewed First Peter 5:10 and the view I had of my physical situation, and He did it when I studied First Peter a second time! Yes, He is gracious enough to allow us to learn a second time, or third, fourth, or fiftieth.

I used the Blue Letter Bible website to look up the biblical meanings of each of the action words that God promises to do in First Peter 5:10:

The Greek word for "perfect" is:
katartiz (verb): to render, i.e. to fit, sound, complete:
(1) to mend (what has been broken or rent), to repair;
(2) to fit out, equip, put in order, arrange, adjust;
(3) ethically: to strengthen, perfect, complete, make one what he ought to be [9]

This sounded so good to me. I admit that I never got

past the first part, "to mend (what has been broken), to repair. All I wanted to know in that moment was that I would be healed such that I could put it all behind me and move on. I expected and presumed that I wouldn't feel pain, not after I was healed, and most certainly not after three years! While I desperately wanted instant and miraculous physical healing, the Lord had something else in mind for me.

Patience.

Perseverance.

Trust in Him and His timing.

I was being challenged to exercise my faith muscles. None of us really wants this, but in the life of a maturing Christian, it is a vital step in the process to maturity. It was evident in the life of Paul. He grew in patience and perseverance from the things he went through. He declared in the book of Philippians that he had learned to be content in every circumstance. Paul learned that God's strength is perfected in weakness.

The Greek word for "confirm" is: st'riz verb:

(1) to make stable, place firmly, set fast, fix;

(2) to strengthen, make firm;

(3) to render constant, confirm, one's mind. [10]

Interestingly, I always saw the words in First Peter 5:10

as a progression or ladder. First perfecting (restoration is the word used in other versions of the Bible), then confirmation, then strengthening, and finally establishing. I don't think it will be a surprise to find out which part of the definition I focused on. Just the first part, and I was only thinking physically. I expected that my unstable ankle was being made stable, firmly set, fixed, and firm.

If I had chosen to read a little more diligently or prayerfully, I might have seen that what Peter meant was not about the physical things, but about spiritual things. It was about becoming strong, fixed, and stable in thought and conviction. This was definitely something that these Christians would need in the face of heavy persecution.

Sadly, I needed it too, but I was so intent on what I wanted. I truly needed to be firm in my understanding of the purpose of trials, and the character of God, but the shock, sadness, desperation and pain had a funny way of skewing things.

The word "strengthen" in Greek is "stheno (verb): to make strong, strengthen; of one's soul",[11] and the word "establish" in Greek is "themelio to lay the foundation, to found; to make stable, establish".[12]

As I said, I was in a place where I wasn't seeing clearly, so I really only took these verses in the literal sense, physically for me. I even prayed for the Lord to supernaturally remove my hardware. I believed He could do that.

When studying the Bible, context is everything, and there was a reason that Peter spoke these particular words to this particular audience. I had interpreted them incorrectly.

That became evident to me after I studied First and Second Peter at a different time, with a different group of ladies, fifteen months after my accident, and a full year after completing the first study of First Peter. During that time, I had a HUGE a-ha moment.

I see now that my understanding or interpretation of First Peter 5:10 was viewed through my deep longing for physical restoration, for strength in my physical body, for my ankle, foot, joint, and ligaments to essentially return to exactly how they operated before they were broken, before there was hardware or trauma. I had interpreted the Scriptures through a lens that I've only just come to understand lately.

Throughout my recovery, I believed that my lot in life was not to have stiffness, occasional pain, and physical limitation even though I have a plate and screws in my ankle! I had an expectation that I would experience full physical restoration to the point that I wouldn't feel any residual effects of the shattered bone, torn ligaments, displaced ankle, or surgery needed to realigned the bones.

What I didn't understand or choose to accept, is that

maybe the residual effects that I have been experiencing aren't all bad. They serve as a reminder of all that God has brought me through. Perhaps it helps me to remain dependent on Him.

I'm glad that my understanding of First Peter 5:10 has changed because I am more in awe of God's wisdom and purpose in my pain, loss, grief, suffering, and confusion. I am more thankful.

The work God wanted to do through it all was to "perfect, confirm, strengthen and establish" me *in my faith*. He wanted to realign my belief in Him, the sovereign Almighty God. He wanted to reveal Himself to me through my shattering experience, to crush my pride, to provide in ways that only He could, and to re-set my theology.

Here's my journal entry as this truth began to take hold:

It has occurred to me that I might not have heard you correctly, Lord – but my expectation was so high that what I heard was full healing – and I thought that meant it would be as if my accident didn't happen. Is it possible that First Peter 5:10 has to do with my faith rather than with my physical healing?

(Journal, May 1, 2020)

Before my accident, I couldn't understand someone who suffers with chronic pain. I didn't know what it feels like to have depression knocking at the door, and I had no way to relate to someone who has suffered sudden loss. Now I do. Not perfectly, but a lot more than I did before. In my journey of recovery, my thinking has changed drastically. I didn't know the level of pride, entitlement, and immaturity I was walking in, but I do now, and I'm thanking the Lord for ridding me of it one day at a time.

While my ankle is fully healed and I have limitations - I have hardware, I developed arthritis, and plantar fasciitis. Now it doesn't seem to matter to me that it be as if it never happened. I am gaining faith and strength in my soul. I have come to the place of thanking God in the circumstances, yes, even for the circumstances. Here are my thoughts:

Father, I think I have had a massive revelation but I want to be sure. I am thinking that First Peter 5:10 was never about physical, though you have healed my foot so that it operates as it did before - you are healing and realigning me - laying the proper foundation for my theology - the true gospel. Not anything added. It's about denying ourselves for the sake of others, bearing up with others' weaknesses, and allowing others to bear us up. It's about suffering with faith and a good attitude - endurance, encouragement.

(Journal, May 6, 2020)

It makes sense that the result of being perfected is to

become secure and firm in Christ. We gain a deeper trust in Him. Importantly, we have a testimony of how God met us, cared for us, and sustained us in the trial, which when shared with others, brings courage, hope, and faith.

In the first go-round with these Scriptures, I was interpreting them literally. After a second pass, I understand that spiritual strengthening is truly what God was after.

There's a saying in the world - "what doesn't kill you makes you stronger" - and though it's not biblical, I think there's something to be said in that. When we walk hand in hand with God through our trials, not turning away or rejecting Him for them, but cooperating with the Holy Spirit, I believe we do come out stronger. We become stronger in our conviction of who God is, and stronger in our connection with the Lord. When we overcome something challenging with God, there is power in that.

It is the Holy Spirit who leads us "through" these trials, just as the Shepherd is with the one who "walks through the valley of the shadow of death" (Psalm 23:4a). We go through life, and the hard things in life. We cannot avoid them, but the great thing is that there is a process of strengthening that the Lord promises as we go "through" them, and one of the best truths is that the Lord is with us.

James said, "the testing of your faith produces endurance .... mature and complete not lacking anything" (James 1:2, CSB). I think this is truly the purpose of trials and difficulties. Being made firm, solid, and steadfast in our faith will give us the endurance we need to carry us through the next trial. Jesus did say, "In the world you will have tribulation" (John 16:33), so we must come to the place of accepting that. Trouble is part of life. Difficulty is part of life, but it doesn't have to take us down or out, because when we go through it with Christ, we come out stronger and more solid. We are able to stand through the next difficult season.

As I write this, I think of the many times I simply wanted to forego suffering, pain and loss, but it was in those times that I felt the Lord's presence, comfort and peace the most. In fact, there have been times lately that I have remembered with fondness, the many hours and days of solitude in my recovery when I heard the Lord's voice so clearly. If that's what it takes to experience true communion and intimacy with the Lord, then it's worth it. Hard. But worth it.

My prayer these days is to remind myself of the words of the Scriptures, and to thank the Lord for all that He did in me, in my mind and in my soul. I can see the fruit of this season, the depth of the intimacy, and the joy of knowing that God purposes to grow me up, to change my character so that I will reflect Christ more and more. This is the truth for all Christians, whatever we go through. This journal entry declares what I was coming to understand:

I'm saying it, Lord. Thank you – since I moved to Mt.

Forest – what a season of tremendous learning, maturing, challenge, faith building, and so much in the hidden, quiet place of my heart, with you. If all of this hadn't happened, I wouldn't know what I know now. What a battle to stay focused on Christ in the middle of physical and emotional pain – not seeking to understand or make sense of it, but trusting you. You know what you're doing. The goal isn't just about physical or emotional healing – the goal is transformation, and that's an inside out job. Wow.

(Journal, July 21, 2021)

In every hard season, there may be a Scripture to hang onto. If not, we can wait and pray, asking the Lord for a word, for a Scripture for our specific circumstance. Whatever the season of suffering, fiery trial, sudden shift, or life difficulty we face, we can find comfort and life in the Scriptures. We can hang on to them, study them, learn from them, and watch God do a work in and through us.

It's very possible to misinterpret the Scriptures in the depth of our sorrow and pain. That's okay. We are all in process and we are all learning as we go. God is good. He promised that the Holy Spirit would guide us into all truth, so at some point or another, we will come to know the truth, and it will set us free (John 8:32). It's important to be open enough to hear what God might want to say to us, and do in us, as we continue enduring and persevering in the middle of difficulties.

QUESTIONS:

1. In your life, can you recall a time that a specific Scripture jumped out at you, and once you were able to get it on the inside of you, it offered you a profoundly strengthening understanding of who God is and what He might be up to in your life?

2. Have you ever considered that some particular theological concept you have been taught could be entirely wrong, that it actually misrepresents the character of God? If not, ask the Holy Spirit to enlighten you in any area that you are not believing accurately.

3. What Scriptures are you hanging onto in this season of your life? Is there one that seems to be coming to your mind more often now than in the past, such that you have a totally new understanding of it that you didn't have before?

TWELVE

ENCOURAGE YOURSELF IN THE LORD

And David was greatly distressed; for the people spake of stoning him, because the soul of all the people was grieved, every man for his sons and for his daughters: but David encouraged himself in the Lord his God.
(1 Samuel 30:6, KJV).

David was in a very alarming and difficult situation. Knowing the character of God, he knew that he needed to encourage or strengthen himself in the Lord to get through what he was facing. This was David, the one who penned a great many Psalms of lament and praise, and who wrote songs to calm King Saul. I love how the Scripture says he encouraged himself in the Lord.

Take note: it does not say that he encouraged himself in food, drink, people, or any form of entertainment. He encouraged himself in the Lord God. What a great principle and practice that we too can adopt in our times of difficulty, stoning or not!

Of all the things I've noticed as I've read over my journals in the early days and months of my recovery, it would have to be that I did rehearse Scripture. I did encourage myself in the Lord, and I did give thanks in my circumstance. It was through this accident and subsequent months of couch recovery alone with Him that God could do a work in me that He could not have done at any other time in my life. After all, He is interested in developing our character in all seasons of life.

Here's something to think about: God desires to show us a part of His character at a time when nothing seems to make sense, at a time when we are most in need of answers. While no one enjoys hearing the following verse in moments of tragedy or deep pain, it is profoundly true. It is a very good thing to remember. It can take time to believe, but looking back, it will become a reality.

"And we know that for those who love God all things work together for good, for those who are called according to his purpose." (Romans 8:28)

Does God really mean all things? That's what it says. All things, including the thing we never wanted or expected, the thing we would rather not have happened - the very thing causing us so much pain, heartache, anger, trauma, and suffering. James exhorted that it is the testing of our faith that develops perseverance (James1:2). I know this to be true. If we let the trial finish its work - and that takes time.

I say to myself and to all Christians in a struggle or difficult time: encourage yourself in the Lord. The worst thing to do would be to turn our backs on Him. He's not turning His back on us. He is with us, willing to help us as we reach out to Him in our deepest valleys.

In my couch time, my desire was to use the trial well, to trust the Lord in it, despite the fact that it was painful, confusing, shocking, and not what I wanted. I did expect it to be over quickly; a short term suffering was something I felt that I could handle with the Lord. Declaring and writing "I can do all things through Christ who gives me strength" encouraged me.

Writing out the first few verses in James 1 and the first chapter of First Peter reminded me that I wasn't alone in my suffering. Trying to understand the words "endurance", "perseverance", and "joy" kept my mind occupied, and solidified for me that there was nowhere else for me to turn to make some sense out of the situation. There had to be a purpose in it all.

I prayed prayers of surrender, of trust, and of love for the Lord and His faithfulness because no matter what, He is good. Turning bitter and angry just wasn't an option for me. I knew that wouldn't be good for me or my healing.

I had to accept what was. I didn't do that well, but over

time I began to accept my new reality. This thing happened to me. I didn't want it. I sure didn't expect it. But God is still good, and He is with me.

When the trials of life blind side us, sometimes it doesn't help to hear what others think about it, that is, what they perceive to be the reason for the trial. I had two friends who felt that I was being disciplined, or even chastened for disobedience. How I was in disobedience, I couldn't discern or figure out.

One friend told me that my healing would be complete when I learned all the lessons the Lord had for me. That was a bitter pill to swallow. I was certainly learning some lessons, but I know that I have a lifetime of lessons ahead of me. I haven't arrived yet. I'm still a work in progress, and the Lord isn't finished with me.

Another friend recounted a story of how shepherds in Israel broke the leg of sheep that wander, so that they don't wander anymore. She said that is what the Lord had done to me. That was pretty harmful to me. It painted Jesus as a cruel shepherd, and it seemed as though I was being punished.

I still don't know why I believed that story. It goes against the character of God. But I was seeking for answers as to why I had hurt myself so badly, and why I was in such a sad, lonely, and painful place.

After fifteen months, I searched out that story to discover if it was actually true. Derek kindly reminded me that in an agrarian society, the shepherd would never want to cause injury to his sheep. After all, they are his livelihood. Furthermore, that injured animal would become easy prey to predators.

That story is a myth. The awful thing is that it has circulated through the church. It makes me sad to think of others who have believed it - it is a complete misrepresentation of shepherds, and ultimately our Good Shepherd.

Once I chose to accept the truth, I began to rehearse the truth about my good Shepherd. Psalm 23 became a go-to verse for me. Jesus, our Shepherd knows what we need and He was the one who knew that I needed a season of rest from all of my former activity.

My friends had good intentions, but their advice and perspective was not helpful. We really do need to seek the Lord for His perspective when bad things happen. We need to be like a Berean and check everything out against the Word of God. It's not wise to just take someone else's word or explanation for our suffering, regardless of how sincere they are. Well meaning Christians, our closest friends, even mentors and pastors, can be wrong, as they can be guessing at what the Lord is doing.

The Lord doesn't always reveal to us what He is doing in the midst of our difficulties. But when we look back, we can see where and how He was at work. Early in my recovery, I did ask the Lord for help. These are the words in my journal:

How do I stay joyful, content, and in peace Lord?

This is how I feel the Holy Spirit answered me,

"Stay in communion with me. Read the Word and worship. Embrace moments, give compliments, encourage others (those I bring to you). Trust me. Every day. All day."
(Journal, December 31, 2019)

This was such practical advice. It was very helpful and something that I could do. Embracing moments is quite radical since we all live planning the next thing. We are programmed culturally for this, but to live in the moment and to encourage others changes our perspective. It frees us up to simply enjoy what the day brings, and if it's hard, to cling to our Saviour Jesus Christ.

As time went on and things seemed to be taking forever to heal, and I couldn't do the things I used to do, I got a bit of an attitude with the Lord. I simply couldn't see why I had to endure physical pain and suffering for so long. While I thought that, I also thought about the pain and suffering Jesus Christ endured on my behalf, to grant me a pardon for all my sins.

I also thought about people I know who live with chronic pain daily, something until now I couldn't personally relate to. It takes a lot of strength, courage, and faith to keep connected to the Lord and people, with joy, when suffering with physical pain. As a friend of mine says, "pain grounds us to this earth". It can become hard to look to Jesus, to His purposes, and to His love, because pain screams for relief.

Needless to say, this trial was truly humbling to me. Landing on my butt at a time when my props had already been knocked out certainly got my attention. I was captive to the Lord in those hours, days, and months sitting on the couch. Some days I did have pity parties and I did want the sympathy of others, but in and through it all, I see that I also did what David did - I encouraged myself in the Lord. We all can, in any season, whatever the circumstance. It's a choice. It's an exercise of faith. It's all about deciding whether we believe God and what He says about Himself.

People can be a source of encouragement in times of difficulty. Scriptures sent at just the right time, a worship song that seems to reach our heart, a meal, a visit, or a phone call can speak volumes to us. They are all wonderful, but they will not be the norm every hour of our time of suffering. There will be many hours and days we find ourselves alone in grief, sorrow, anger, and shock. In the really tough times, turn to the Lord. He can be our greatest source of encouragement.

When we remember that the Lord is as close as the mention of His name, and that He is close to the brokenhearted, our eyes and hearts turn away from ourselves and our situations. The Holy Spirit is our greatest encourager, counselor, comforter and friend (John 14:26, AMP). He will be so real to all who allow Him in. While the encouragement from people helps, the comfort of God goes much deeper, and it has the capacity to heal our deepest hurts and answer our toughest questions.

Romans 8:28 says, "And we know that for those who love God all things work together for good, for those who are called according to his purpose." I did not see the good in the middle of the shock, pain, confusion and trauma, but over time, I certainly did. God began to change me from the inside out.

He changed my thinking, my attitudes, and my very heart, and He did it fairly quickly. I can remember telling a friend in early February - just after the two month mark - that I was actually thankful that my break and recovery happened in Mt. Forest. Being in a new community with virtually no one to offer support and comfort, I came to know the Lord in a whole new way. He was so close to me, and His voice was loud at times.

God was not finished with me at the two month mark, let alone the three year mark. I still need to remind myself to encourage myself in the Lord, to come to Him daily for intimate connection, refreshing, and His living water. I'm so thankful for the changes in my life as a result of breaking my ankle in the midst of an already lonely season of life. I am just not the same person anymore!

This is my encouragement to anyone who is going through deep waters, when feeling broken and confused: Keep going. Keep encouraging yourself in the Lord. Keep hanging onto the Father, and He will do something in you that you never expected or could have foreseen.

He will use the painful trial to refine you into a more beautiful reflection of Jesus Christ. Please note however, that this happens when we stay connected to Him. It is vitally important not to focus on the struggle, misery, and pain. Focus on Jesus.

QUESTIONS:

1. When you are going through the valley of disappointment and pain, does Romans 8:28 irritate you or give you comfort? Why?

2. Describe a time when someone in your life tried to explain the reason behind your suffering, which you later discovered didn't line up with the character of God or with Scripture. How did you uncover the truth?

3. In what ways can you "encourage yourself in the Lord"?

THIRTEEN

BE GENTLE ON YOURSELF

The title of this chapter came from a meme that I found on a friend's FaceBook page soon after I moved to Mt. Forest. It was very helpful to me as I grieved the many losses and changes in my life. The full wording was:

It takes as long as it takes. Be gentle on yourself.

I had made a drawing of it and taped it to my wall as a reminder that some things take time to heal. For me, at the time I read it, I was experiencing emotional pain. I had been contemplating these words for months prior to that fateful day in December, 2019 when I broke my ankle.

It became one of my "go-to" thoughts as I journeyed through physical healing and restoration, as well as my emotional and spiritual struggles. Through that first year after my surgery, I needed to be reminded to be gentle on myself.

When life as we know it stops, it's not easy, especially for those of us who are type "A" personalities. Being gentle on ourselves is actually one of the most necessary things we can do when life suddenly shifts in a direction we weren't prepared for. The change is so massive, it simply can't be processed right away. It can only be worked through little by little.

Though others around us may try to rush us and our own expectations may cause us to push ourselves to get back to normal, that's really not helpful. It can even be harmful. As I read back over my journals, here are a few entries that indicate that I was expecting far too much of myself in the early stages of my recovery:

I am still not settling down. I'm itching to "do", to get better fast. I have got to accept reality and make the most of it. Impatience needs to go, in Jesus name. Immaturity. Lack of trust. Not getting my way. Things not going the way I want. These emotions are similar to shaking my fist at God.
(Journal, December 12, 2019 - 9 days post surgery)

I'm pushing too hard – not being realistic. I can't possibly drive an hour yet. It will come. I need to rest and take it all one day at a time. I shouldn't be making plans. I have made progress; I'm down to one foam pad in my boot cast. So celebrate,

*enjoy, think about it. But move on: get my mind off myself and
my situation.*

(Journal, December 21, 2019 -18 days post surgery)

These were still very early days and I was already trying
to make plans and push myself beyond the limitations I
had. I could not and would not accept that it was a very
real and distinct possibility that my ankle would not feel
normal for a full twelve months.

Thankfully, I came to recognize that my restlessness
and frustration was actually hurting me. I was pushing
myself to try to gain healing, rather than allowing God
to heal me in His time. I was not exercising patience, but
rather demonstrating a profound amount of impatience.
Even though I remembered the words in the book of James
about endurance and patience, I wasn't doing a good job
at either. At one point, I was trying to keep my leg down
- not elevated - for longer than five or ten minutes even as
it got purple and tingly, and was uncomfortably inflamed.

In that time, I heard the Holy Spirit speak this into
my heart, "Are you trying to punish yourself?" I have been
learning that pushing can become punishing, but patience
is proof of self love. Not only that, it's proof of trust in
God's timing.

As the book of Ecclesiastes teaches, there's a time and
season for everything under heaven. For me, there was to
be a time to rest and a time to move. I was trying to do

both at the same time, and that just didn't work. It caused me physical pain, made me frustrated at myself, and at times, I was angry with the Lord.

Regarding rest, Scripture teaches, "The Lord is my shepherd. I shall not want. He makes me lie down in green pastures. He leads me beside still waters. He restores my soul" (Psalm 23:1-2). You may find different Scriptures more fitting to your unique experience, but there was no doubt in my mind that the Lord was calling me to be still and to rest, both physically as well as mentally and emotionally. He had been calling me into it even before we moved.

Getting used to a totally different life takes time. Healing takes time. Getting our minds around the significance of the change takes time. Yet, embracing the process of healing, and allowing God to lead us is actually very freeing. I can say that now in retrospect, but while I was in it, I didn't quite see it that way. We absolutely must work through the pain, grief and confusion.

Importantly, we must also go at our own pace, not in line with what anyone else says or expects of us. We must get past the denial and address what is reality. It is entirely possible for us to have unrealistic expectations on ourselves regarding how long it will take until life returns to some semblance of "normal". It's important to realize that in advance.

Unrealistic expectations are just that. Unrealistic! They

are not based in reality. I discovered that the longer we hang onto them, the more angry and frustrated we become. That's why the Lord needs to "make" the sheep lie down in green pastures. It's important for us to get to the place where we live in moments, and appreciate progress or any forward movement, no matter how small. Getting stuck in grief and pain isn't a good place to be. It means we are not moving forward; we are stuck in one place. Actually, it means we are moving backwards.

I have learned that there is an end to the intensity of the emotions we experience. It is a process that takes time. Turning to the Lord, giving thanks for any little thing in the circumstance, and maintaining communication and connection with the Lord, causes that forward movement in our ability to see things as they are - realistically. When normal has shifted, things may not return to the old normal, because when God is at work, He's doing a new thing.

Letting others help does take a weight off, and asking for help means we let others into our journey, and this lessens our frustration. I had to learn to be gentle on myself, and I believe others can learn it also. I exhort these things from my own personal experience: let others help; ask for help; be gentle on yourself. I wanted to drive when I wasn't even off crutches, in the winter where snow and ice are slippery. That's why I put my foot down for longer periods of time.

These were not gentle strategies. They were hurtful, harmful, and rooted in impatience. I wanted my healing to hurry up and it was only at the beginning - less than three weeks in. Here are two more journal entries that indicate where I was at:

Lots of tears today. Reality of my situation. This isn't a quick fix. Slow and steady progress. I didn't want to go to church. I just can't fake it – I'm weary.
(Journal, December 29, 2019)

Yesterday I was laughing, positive, feeling great. Today not so much. I didn't sleep well. I put my foot down and had pain. I am getting tired of all of this. Last night I felt like I had accepted life as it is... but today, I feel fat, dirty, grubby and sad. I'm reading James to get my mind off me. Thank you Lord that you are with me – your presence is around me. I want to wait on you, to grow, to learn and to be stretched. To be patient with myself. Be kind. The Lord's response - "Trust me. This is going to take some time."
(Journal, January 3, 2020 - one month after surgery)

"Trust me. This is going take some time". These were the Lord's words to me. Like I said, it's so important to have God's truth and perspective in seasons we've never been in before, when our own expectations and the expectations of those around us can press in on us. We exercise a huge amount of faith when we simply trust God right where we are, trusting that He knows what He's doing, and that He is always at work.

I can remember someone telling me to get off the narcotics quickly lest I become addicted. So I attempted that. That wasn't good advice! I suffered when I didn't take the medication. Who's to say that I'd get addicted? I didn't. They do serve a purpose - pain control. Why was I trying to be a martyr when God hadn't called me to do that.

Here's a journal entry when I was having a hard time with my reality:

I need to turn my eyes on Jesus because focusing inward doesn't produce anything helpful. The pain is real and I'm tired. Father, I come now to your throne of mercy. I need your grace. In this moment. To endure another day, another hour. I'm so thankful to be walking and each day is easier – But O God, this feels so long and lonely. I know you are with me. I'm hurting physically.

I guess I thought or hoped it was not going to hurt so much. Or last so long. So I accept reality again. I'm not quite at three months. Takes six months for ligaments to heal and swelling to go down. That means I'm not quite half way. So day by day living – that's what I must come into. And not concern myself with how long, or anyone's expectations on timing.

(Journal, February 15, 2020)

All of us are tempted to hurry our situation or to set goals that aren't realistic. Faith isn't only about believing for what isn't seen. Faith is also trusting that God knows what He's doing and that He will bring about the healing in His time, not our time. We live in an instant and fast food culture, but God is not limited to our timing. He is not limited in anything.

I didn't know that the time God chose to heal me was actually so far above mere physical healing. He was about healing my thoughts, my emotions, and my understanding of who I am in Him. I had to learn that I am not what I do for Him or for others. I had to get to a place of deep dependence, restful abiding, no more striving, and anyone who's like me will too!

Learning to be gentle on oneself can seem really hard. This culture and our expectations scream at us to get going, to hurry up, and to press on, but sometimes the better thing we can do is to take our time, accept our limitations, and do what we can do, and refrain from doing what is harmful. After all, it takes as long as it takes, and we don't actually know how long it will take.

Surrender and acceptance aren't weakness. They are trust - trust in an all knowing God, an all powerful God, a caring God. At Celebrate Recovery, we read the Serenity Prayer every week. There's a lot of truth in it, truth that is worth thinking about. I've included a portion of the prayer that I needed to remember in my recovery and still do at times:

> God, grant me the serenity to accept
> the things I cannot change;
> courage to change the things I can;
> and wisdom to know the difference.
> Living one day at a time;
> enjoying one moment at a time;
> accepting hardships as the pathway to peace...
> Reinhold Neibuhr

QUESTIONS:

1. How do you feel when you read "It takes as long as it takes. Be gentle on yourself." ? The thoughts or emotions that bubble up as you think about that statement may be quite telling in where you are at in your own recovery journey and with your ability to trust God.

2. Have you been aware of your desire to move things along faster than is necessary, faster than is helpful? Are you listening to other people's voices about how soon you should be moving forward after a life-changing season that was full of pain, grief, and suffering?

3. Do you think the concept of living one day at a time is realistic in our current day and age? Why, or why not? Have you ever tried it? Why, or why not?

FOURTEEN

PITY IS NO PARTY

There's a saying we've all heard, and that is, "misery loves company", but the truth is: misery doesn't make good company at all!

One of the things I learned through my recovery journey is that a lot of the talking I was doing was about myself, my pain, my suffering, what happened to me. I believe there is absolutely a need for that, for a time. I process things by talking about them, and my husband is amazing at simply listening and letting me yak up a storm about any little or big thing. However, several months into the aftermath of not weight bearing for nine weeks, learning to walk, doing physiotherapy, and experiencing pain most days for months, followed by the growth of a ganglion cyst a year later, I still found that I was talking about myself a lot! With anyone, and everyone.

It's natural to want to commiserate, vent, and share what's going on with others who will listen. After a while, however, it can become all consuming. To be so self-focused gets tiring for others, not to mention very boring. I admit that my situation and all the gory details of what I was going through were topics of discussion at our dining room table, with friends, and with my adult children every time they called. Every time!

I'm a little embarrassed to admit that when I wasn't asked, "how are you doing?", I thought that the person on the other end of the phone didn't care. My resultant emotion was anger, frustration and grief.

Negative emotions and thoughts aren't healthy or helpful when they aren't based in truth. I couldn't possibly perceive that the other person didn't care by the questions they did or didn't ask. Talking about what we're going through, and wanting to vent is absolutely warranted and okay, for a time, but doing so incessantly for months or even years on end can be too much.

From my experience, I have learned that it is not helpful for the one suffering to linger or focus too long on their pain. I suppose I was looking for sympathy or understanding, but what I wasn't thinking about was what anyone else was going through.

Part of my lament in the early days of my couch sitting was that I felt like some of my close friends weren't there for me. Looking back, I can see that I expected them to be there, and when they weren't, I was deeply disappointed. Sadly, I was so focused on myself that I never even considered what might have been going on in their lives. What struggles or hardships were they enduring? One day I asked the Lord, "Where are my peeps?", and "Why won't anyone sit on my ash pile with me?" I was so low, feeling so alone, and all I wanted was people to be with me to comfort me.

God knew that although this was what I wanted, this was not what I needed. He began to work in me a deep dependence on Him, rather than co-dependence on people. He began to teach me to listen to His voice, and less to the world's voices, and even more importantly, less to the voice of my flesh.

I recently completed a Bible study titled *No Other gods* by Kelly Minter. I find her words do a really great job of summarizing what I was going through:

There are seasons when you are surrounded by the people you need, and the relationships with your family and friends are firing on all cylinders. But there are also seasons when, regardless of intent, the people from whom you often draw strength may not be able to give it to you. It's in these times of relational scarcity when we discover the true Source of our strength and contentment. [13]

This is so very true. God is our best and truest source

of strength and contentment, not people. Now I see that I had put my friends in a position that God Himself intended to occupy in my life.

I'm not saying that having friends and support is wrong, by no means! But ultimately, our support and comfort should first and mostly come from the Lord. There were people who came to visit on occasion, and I was grateful for their visits. Some drove an hour from Owen Sound. My sister Liz and my mom came from Toronto, which is two hours away.

On one occasion, however, in my lonely and miserable place, I became overwhelmed and lost sight of the good in my life. I was sitting in my favourite place - the couch - on Boxing Day 2019. It was a dull winter's day. As was their daily practice, Derek and Charles had left to work on the apartment around 9am and would be home at 6:30pm. I had already spent what felt like a thousand hours alone, and the Christmas holidays felt bleaker this time. Our eldest son Derek Jr. was in England visiting his girlfriend. This was his first Christmas away from home. We hadn't seen him since October and wouldn't see him again until February. I really missed him.

Over the entire Christmas break, I had been with family on just one day when we drove to Toronto for lunch on December 25. Other than that, I spent every day alone.

On this particular day, the dullness of the weather and with my sad thoughts and feelings swirling, my sense of loneliness began to increase exponentially. While sitting in the quiet, in pain and feeling very sorry for myself, I felt pulled. I can only describe it as what seemed to be like claws of darkness. In the moment, it didn't feel evil or scary. I felt invited to just crawl into bed, take some pain pills, pull the covers over my head, and shut the world out.

I remember that I was also somewhat frustrated that I still had one foam pad in my boot cast, and I just needed it to be gone in order for me to get the boot cast off at the six week mark. This was three and a half weeks in. Oh, how impatient I was!

I really don't know how long my thoughts went in that dark direction, but there was a moment when I knew that this was neither helpful nor healthy for me. It was then that I decided to put on some worship music on. I needed to change my focus, turn my thoughts away from the invitation to darkness, and get my mind onto God. I had already taken medication for pain, and had a nap that day. I didn't need more pills or sleep, but that is what I felt drawn to do.

As I listened to some of my favourite songs, I actually couldn't sing. This was a big clue that something was very wrong, because I love to sing, and I normally sing quite loudly when I am worshiping the Lord. But that day, in those moments, I couldn't sing. I could barely even speak the words of the songs. I moved my lips but no sound came out! I kept playing songs one after another, sometimes several times over: songs about the goodness of God, about His love, and about His power.

Eventually, things started to lighten up as I turned my eyes and my thoughts onto truth, onto God, and off of my situation and my emotional pain. In time, I could sing a few words, and finally the tears started to run down my face. The light was getting in, the truth was penetrating the darkness, and I began to feel the presence and comfort of God.

The final song I played was "Overcomer", by Mandisa, which I was able to sing along with. After rehearsing the truth that I am an overcomer, I declared, "I can do all things through Christ who gives me strength". Here's my journal entry:

> *Breakthrough! Took a nap in the day. Took pills for pain.*
> *Then I got very lonely and sad. I cried and then listened to*
> *worship songs to get my mind into truth. Then I had the*
> *courage to take the last pad out from the heel of my boot cast –*
> *and I could put my foot down all the way. I reached my goal!*
> *(Journal, December 26, 2019)*

My sorrow turned into joy, and from that point on, I recognized the very real temptation and work of the enemy, the devil. This is why, in my earlier chapters, I strongly suggest reading Scripture and staying focused on the Lord. I walked through a dark place, but the Holy

Spirit pulled me out of it and into the light.

One of the best pieces of advice I heard when I was part of the Celebrate Recovery ministry was that a person in pain should help another person who is suffering or in pain. The purpose of that is to replace self-focused thoughts with thoughts of another. Having too much of our thoughts focused on our own suffering can be harmful.

By comparison, intentionally choosing to look to Jesus, setting our minds on things above, and reaching out to others, is beneficial. It offers a whole new perspective on life.

So, that is what I began to do. I started writing blogs again to express how I was feeling, to share how God was meeting me, and to encourage others. This helped me to remind myself of the goodness of God in my difficulty. I started creating encouragement cards for others. It gave me tremendous joy to anonymously bless and share God's truth with people from our church congregation. I also made more of an effort to make meals for Derek and me, to clean up afterwards, all the while wheeling around in the rented wheelchair. This blessed Derek and simplified his life a little bit. It also gave me joy!

I had also started a new hobby called "diamond painting" which gave me hours of entertainment every day. I began to pray and sing worship songs while I worked on my project. I was able to focus on something other than myself, which was good. It was so relaxing and enjoyable to see a piece of art become a reality. This has become a hobby I continue to do today, and I have told many other people about its benefits.

I have found that when I chose to turn my eyes and my focus off of me and my situation, I discovered a sense of peace and joy in thinking beyond myself. While it didn't change my difficult circumstance or shift the physical pain, it did change my outlook. Importantly, I had other things to talk about than myself!

Pity is no party. It really takes us down into places that bring pain and hurt rather than healing. Consider looking to Jesus instead, and let the Holy Spirit lead you into a sacrifice of praise instead.

QUESTIONS:

1. How can you relate to Wendy's story about pity, self-focus, and wanting the sympathy of others? Have you experienced a time when your "peeps" or "props" were not available to you? How did it make you feel?

2. What do you think about the comment, "God didn't give me what I wanted because He knew what I needed"? Have your experienced this in your life? Has God provided what you needed, even though at the time you didn't even know you needed it?

3. If you have experienced the darkness Wendy felt, how did God shine His light to bring you out of it? If you are in a time of deep depression, is there anything you would be willing to try that Wendy shared? Eg. New hobby, worship music, blessing others, looking to God.

FIFTEEN

FEAR IS A LIAR

I find it fascinating to reflect on the things I was thinking about during my recovery. I can remember being absolutely terrified of falling down the stairs on my crutches. In fact, every so often I would imagine myself being launched from the top step to the bottom of the stairs. Because of this, instead of practicing how to crutch up and down the stairs, I did what is commonly known as "bumming".

Every time I went up or down my stairs - which I had to do often to let Sammy out when Derek wasn't home - I slid down to the floor. Then, on my rear end, I scooted along and down the stairs, cleaning the floor of dust and dirt as I went. On the way up, I pulled myself up the stairs in a crab walk, going backwards, with my left leg extended straight out. Then I launched myself into a chair, grabbed my crutches, and made my way over to the wheelchair. It was good for my arm muscles, but rather embarrassing to do in front of anyone who was visiting. Many times I left the front door open so that people could come in on their own.

The idea of falling down the stairs was a reasonable fear since I was new at crutching, but to see myself being launched from the top to the bottom was not even close to a realistic notion. I can't recall exactly when that fear entered my mind, but it seemed to be a very real possibility to me. I thought about it frequently, sometimes once a day. Looking back, I can see that fear had a hold on me, and because of it, I simply refused to even attempt to crutch up or down the stairs.

I was also incredibly worried about slipping on ice when I had to go to follow up appointments from December through February. Since I was using crutches, followed by a cane during these months, I still needed support for walking. I believed that my front door step was enormous, which it isn't. I convinced myself that I couldn't possibly crutch or hop up onto it, especially since it had no hand rail.

Instead, despite the slipperiness of the floor, I came through the garage whenever I had to leave and re-enter our house. In my way of thinking, the two small steps from the garage to the house were do-able. I could hop up or down while placing my hands on both sides of the door frame, or I could use my crutches with Derek ready to catch me if I fell.

It's possible that these fears escalated after I actually did fall in the middle of the night. At 2am, while I was returning from the bathroom, still on painkillers, and in the dark, whilst trying ever so hard to be quiet, my crutches slipped away from me. Just as I entered our bedroom, my crutches went left and right, and I slid down to the floor. I landed with a loud THUD, and none too graceful at that! My rear end hit the floor, with my legs straight out in front of me.

This noise woke Derek up from a very sound sleep, which is never a good idea. It certainly woke me up too! Getting from the floor to standing again was not easy; it took considerable effort. Embarrassing? Yes. It was also pretty scary. I fell! One of my worst fears had been realized! Yet, thankfully, I did not hurt my foot or anything else. The only thing hurt was my pride.

Another crutch mishap happened when they slipped away from me upon my arrival into the kitchen one morning, with Charles as a witness. This time, I put my left foot down, resulting in a squeal from the pain, another dose of fear, and an outburst of tears. In hindsight, and with the help of Charles, I soon learned that I wasn't using the crutches properly, and that I needed to be more careful on the kitchen floor, which was slippery at times.

The fear of falling wasn't unreasonable as I had fallen twice with my crutches, but the idea of being launched from the top of the stairs to the bottom was not conceivably possible. At times, my fears became larger than life.

Fears can also be unknowingly planted in our minds by other people. I recall a well meaning acquaintance telling me of an accident and surgery he had experienced, followed by pain medications and physiotherapy. His advice? "Get off the pain killers quick. You don't want to become addicted." I took that one to heart. How many stories have I heard of people getting addicted to the opiates post surgery.

So I rationed the doses, perhaps even choosing pain over relief, in the minuscule chance that I would get addicted. I wasn't sure that I had a sufficient supply of pills in the bottles as it was. After calling my family doctor for more, I soon learned just how difficult it is to get more opiates, even if I was becoming dependent, which I wasn't.

Another fear I had was this: "Will I have to live with chronic pain the rest of my life?" This one lingered as the pain lingered, and increased after I developed a ganglion cyst. I experienced new pain and discomfort every time I walked, from July through to December, a full year following the first surgery. Thankfully, I was able to have it surgically removed.

Since then, I have developed plantar fasciitis. This is a pain and discomfort that I experience nearly every day, coupled with occasional pain or stiffness in my ankle after lots of activity, or when the barometric pressure changes, especially in the cooler months of the year. I do not know if this will be an on-going condition for years ahead, but I am learning to trust and depend on the Lord while I continue to suffer with physical pain.

I think it's natural to have some fear when our world's been turned upside down. We don't need to condemn ourselves for it. It is a good idea to examine the fears we have since so many of them are quite simply based on lies. It was unreasonable to think that I would be launched from the top step to the bottom, but it wasn't unreasonable to think I might have residual pain for years to come.

Living in fear and in lies of what might be true, but isn't currently true, is something that we must not do as believers in Christ. It leads to increased pain and sorrow, and it can prolong our recovery.

In our times of fear, in our times of pain, grief, sorrow and confusion, we have a choice to make. We can choose to trust in what we see and feel, or we can choose to trust in God. He knows what He is doing in and through every situation. He is working all things for the good of those who love Him (Romans 8:28).

When I am walking in fear and thinking fearful things, I find it helpful to get my mind into truth, that is, biblical truth. Paul wrote to Timothy, saying, "For God has not given us a spirit of fear, but of power and of love and of a sound mind" (2 Timothy 1:7, NKJV). This is something I had to tell myself quite regularly.

When we've had a traumatic event and when our

beliefs about ourselves, God and others shift, we have an enemy who loves to come in with lies to feed our pain, grief and fears. Fear can definitely come in the form of a spirit, that is, a demonic influence on our minds. But because we are in Christ and we can walk in truth, by faith, it doesn't have to stick around. It can leave, and it will leave, in Jesus' name. The Bible says, "perfect love casts out fear" (1 John 4:18). In addition, the Apostle Paul said that the power that raised Jesus from the dead lives in us (Romans 8:11). Be encouraged! We have more power in us than we actually know!

We also have a sound mind. The ESV version of the Bible uses the word "self control" in the place of the words "sound mind". It's not helpful to let our fearful thoughts run away on us. We can and we need to come into truth. We must feed ourselves something better. That's why it is so important to keep praying, to stay in the Bible, and to remind ourselves of truth. "God has not given us a spirit of fear, but of power and of love and of a sound mind."

Each of us experiences our own situations and fears. Isn't it good to know that God's Word is rich with encouragement for each and every thing we go through. God is a personal God. Jesus promised to be with us. The Lord sees and the Lord cares. These are some truths that are helpful to reflect on, even memorize, in times of difficulty:

"I will never leave you nor forsake you."
(Hebrews 13:5b)

"The Lord is near to the brokenhearted."
(Psalm 34:18a)

"...the Father of mercies and God of all comfort, who comforts us in all our affliction."
(2 Corinthians 1:3b-4a)

"fear not, for I am with you;
be not dismayed, for I am your God"
(Isaiah 41:10a)

Whenever I had an issue swirling around and taking over my thoughts, I went to Scripture. I also did some research about it. In my times of prayer, I felt the Lord saying to me, "Do not be discouraged. Do what the doctor says, and do what I say." I wrote out Joshua 1:9 several times because there were days I really needed to remember that the Lord God was with me wherever I was, and wasn't going. He was my very present help in my time of trouble.

When the home physiotherapist came and taught me how to properly go up and down the stairs, using one crutch, and holding onto the hand rail, I became quite proficient at it.

I'm glad to say that the fear associated with falling down

the stairs left. As for the fear of addiction, I discounted it also because I didn't see it being played out in my life. The enormous front step fear? It left also after I built up enough physical strength and confidence with the cane. While on crutches, I continued to use the garage door. I think that was just wise.

Lastly, the chronic pain fear - that one hung on for some time as a real concern. After surgery to remove that ganglion cyst one year and two weeks after the ORIF surgery, I experienced a resurgence of pain which required another six weeks of physiotherapy. This was not related to the cyst removal. It was related to the first surgery.

Even though I continue to experience pain from my injury, and most recently plantar fasciitis, I feel less frustrated and disappointed about it. That's because of how God has changed my view of Him, and my view of suffering.

I can endure it, regardless of whether the residual pain leaves or not. It serves as a reminder of my most intimate times with the Lord when I was on my couch for those many months.

QUESTIONS:

1. Have you considered your own fears, and whether they are reasonable or not? For the bigger than life fears, how are you staying in truth?

2. Do you agree that "fear is a liar"? If not, why not? What do you believe about fear?

3. What are some practical things you can do to reduce or eliminate your fear?

SIXTEEN

FOCUS ON WHAT YOU CAN DO

In the early days of my recovery, I wrote in my journal, "I can do all things through Christ who gives me strength." These words come from the Apostle Paul's words in Philippians 4:13. Since looking back through my journal notes, I see that I wrote it many times on many days, sometimes even many times in one day!

Was that wishful thinking, a positive declaration, or simply a desperate plea to be true? I know I wrote it to encourage myself, and to stay positive. Perhaps I also wrote it to remember that I could do some things in those days of bearing no weight on my foot, living most days on the couch, surrounded by hours of silence, without the physical presence of people.

It's possible it was something I wrote out without thinking about what it meant. Maybe I just wrote it out because that's what I'd been taught - I can do all things through Christ who gives me strength! It's a truth to declare, a promise to proclaim.

As I reflect back on those early days, I realize that I didn't really know what the verse meant. They were good words, hopeful words, and helpful to my desperate heart. But the truth is, I was so very frustrated and sad at the things I could not do anymore. The thing I understood the Lord to be saying clearly to me was: endure, be patient, persevere, and trust Him. As a "do-er", I could see the Lord wasn't overly interested in my "doings".

Instead, He was working on the attitudes of my heart. I have come to discover that the Lord Jesus Christ cares a great deal about our hearts when we walk through difficulties and trials. What is the state of our heart in the middle of troubling times? I have no doubt that He cares about our physical state too, but when we face trials of various kinds, James writes, "consider it joy". Joy is an attitude, not something we do.

We all go through different things. All the trials we go through have the purpose of strengthening our faith, deepening our dependence on Christ, and making us more like Christ. Looking back, we are often able to see His goodness in and through it all. I can say that now. However, in the middle of it, I couldn't see it very clearly, despite my reading those "trial" verses over and over again.

Here is a journal entry when I express my feelings

about what I was going through over two months into my recovery:

Yesterday I was very sad. The thought that what used to bring me joy is now painful was a lot to bear. Walking around Canadian Tire and No Frills hurt a lot. I just got upset, so upset. How long O Lord? I had a hard time moving into a more positive outlook. Acceptance. Reality. I so wanted to make supper or empty the dishwasher but I couldn't.

(Journal, February 10, 2020)

In my mind, "I can do all things through Christ who gives me strength" had to do with what I could do physically. As I shared in earlier chapters, I was thinking I could do this: drive within a month, walk in six or seven weeks, and that everything would be back to "normal" quickly. But unbeknownst to me, these were not the "things" Christ was giving me strength for. He was giving me strength for these things:

Endurance,
patience,
perseverance,
dependence on Him, and,
ears to hear His still small voice.

Those other things? The things I wanted and expected

Christ to give me strength for? They were completely unrealistic "things" at that time. In the midst of difficult seasons, it can be helpful to ask the Holy Spirit this question: "At this time, what are the things that Jesus Christ will give me strength for?"

Our flesh and our heart desperately want to do the things we want to do, when we want to do them. Furthermore, we want Jesus Christ to give us strength to do them, and in the time we expect. There are many things we can do in our own strength, but eventually these things leave us worn out from trying. When Christ gives us strength, we will accomplish what He is asking of us, and what He asks of us might surprise us.

Earlier I told you the story of a woman walking her dog down my street, which prompted me to crumple into a flood of tears at not being able to do that activity anymore. It was that day when I heard the still small voice of God saying,

"Focus on what you can do, not on what you can't do."

In an instant, those words snapped the chains of disappointment and frustration. I wasn't seeing all the things that I could do in my time of being alone, resting, recovering, and healing. One thing we can all do is give thanks. We can choose to have an attitude of gratitude while we endure our difficult circumstances.

Reading the Bible, singing songs, encouraging ourselves in the Lord, and even taking the time to encourage others are all good activities to do while we walk through our valleys. I spent time on creative projects, read countless books, and eventually reached out to others, to find out about their lives.

Although I was physically limited, I could crutch my way to the bathroom, bedroom, kitchen, and the dining room table when Derek had our meals ready. It wasn't long before I could do more than that. Within the first few days of me being home from surgery, a new acquaintance at church suggested we rent a wheelchair. That would give me mobility and help me to do some additional things.

That was something we did, and what a blessing it was! Having a wheelchair gave me enough mobility to get myself a coffee or water, and to even make a light meal for myself. In addition, I could wash a couple of dishes, empty the dishwasher, and help prepare supper for when Derek would come home to cook it at 6:30pm.

The beauty of our new home was that most of our living space was on one floor, with no stairs. We had large entrance ways between the kitchen, living room, and dining room. This opened up a whole new world of "I can's" to me, which helped my overall attitude and outlook on life.

"Success comes in cans not can'ts."
Anonymous

I found that quote long after I experienced the truth of it, but it really fits my "I can" moments. I can recall making our bed for the first time as I crutched my way around it, leaning my crutches against the bed, and standing on one foot. It felt really good to be able to do that. I remember the first time I scrubbed the kitchen sink until it sparkled, and how happy that made me feel. I know that sounds weird. Moving from an "I can't" to an "I can" attitude is life changing from the moment we choose to embrace it.

In that time, I also discovered a craft called "diamond art" which I talked about in an earlier chapter. I was able to set it up on the dining room table and leave it there to come back to several times a day. It certainly gave my mind something else to focus on. Working at it gave me joy and a sense of accomplishment. What I didn't know at the time is that all creative activities have a positive effect on a person's brain, releasing dopamine and serotonin, also known as the "feel good" chemicals.

Here's another "I can" story: When I realized we wouldn't be attending the Christmas church service in which I had agreed to read a story, I decided to create a video and record myself reading the story instead. Though I couldn't be at the service in person, I could participate in a whole different way. It's a good thing this idea came to me as I don't think I would have been able to stand with my crutches for that long anyway.

This video project allowed me to learn some new

things with my computer, and it occupied several hours of my time. I felt great joy at being able to contribute in that way. I had a lot of fun creating the video and narrating the story of "The Tale of the Three Trees".

Here are some journal entries around that time:

This accident has exposed weaknesses but you O, God have brought me strength.

(Journal, December 28, 2019)

I attempted to put my shoe on out of curiosity – absolutely not a chance. This made me so very sad -- but the Lord says "don't be discouraged. Be patient." Ok. I can practice with bare feet. But the boot will be on until I can fit a shoe. There's just no way around it.

(Journal, January 8, 2020)

Focusing on what we "can" do really does bring a measure of joy, a sense of accomplishment, and a focus away from the "can'ts". For me, practicing my physiotherapy exercises with bare feet when I couldn't get a shoe on, and using the strength I did have to do simple tasks, made a huge difference to my outlook on life.

When we gave back the wheelchair after two months of use, I needed to discover other things I could possibly do. Even though I couldn't walk without a cane or crutch, I could put some weight on my foot. On one particular day, the old saying: "necessity is the mother of invention" popped into my head. That's when I began to come up with ideas for more "I can's", things that I had been able to do with the help of the wheelchair, but now needed to figure out a new way to do. It was the right time to do so as my in-home physiotherapist had told me to stop using the wheelchair as a "crutch". He began to push me to use one crutch or the cane instead. I needed to push myself also.

I began to practice standing in the middle of the kitchen, with my arms spread out. I would reach over to the coffee maker, pour my coffee, then pivot, carrying my cup. Reaching over to the island, I would dress up my coffee, pivot again, and reach over to open the fridge to return the cream. Then I would hop along, moving my coffee cup with me around the island until I was near the dining room. Taking a small side table for support, I could than balance my cup on the table. With a hand on either side of the table, I pushed it along the floor until I reached the living room rug. Then I could support myself by hanging onto furniture, placing my drink on other side tables, all the while hopping or limping, and passing the drink along until I finally made it to the living room couch. It became a bit of a game, one which I came to enjoy and laugh at.

Another creative "I can" was to pour my water into a re-useable container with a lid, and drop it into the pocket of my pants, my bathrobe, or whatever clothing I was wearing. Eventually, I got a satchel, and then a backpack to bring items up and down the stairs, or from room to room when I needed them. That way I didn't need to ask for help from Derek. I could do things during the day when he wasn't around. This gave me increased independence, and that felt good! It's amazing what we can discover if we slow down our emotions, relax, and think about it.

Some things will take time before we "can" do them. In the meantime, it helps to "focus on what you can do, not on what you can't do"! Here's a journal entry describing my little victories:

Necessity is the mother of invention. I can now transport drinks with my little table. And I moved a chair down the hallway by pushing it with my stomach while crutching. Now I can put a leg up while sitting in a different chair in the living room. This is progress, victory! I walk around the kitchen with one hand on the counter and it feels good. Each new discovery gives me more confidence and a willingness to try. This is so great.

(Journal, January 27, 2020)

Maybe for you, getting out of bed is the "I can", or taking a shower, or making a phone call, or opening the mail, or making a meal. We all have struggles and difficulties and different challenges. It is so helpful to take the time to discover what we can do, even one thing we find possible to do in our time of suffering. Over time, we will come to realize there are more and more things that we can do. As I wrote in my journal, each new discovery gave me confidence and a willingness to try.

Focus on what you can do, not on what you can't do.

I'm glad for this line. I needed to remind myself of this especially when I first started to go for walks. Prior to my accident, it wasn't unusual for me to walk upwards of an hour. When I first started walking again, I could walk past a few houses, and then I needed to turn around and come home. That line helped me to focus on the "can", not the "can't". This was critical to keep frustration and anger from creeping in. When I could walk around a small block, I celebrated that, and then I tried a bigger block, albeit slowly at times.

Today I am able to do the same length of walks I did prior to the accident, and I have started skating. Some days I have to take time to rest my foot. That's ok. It's progress, and I'm focusing on what I CAN do. It really is a great place to be.

QUESTIONS:

1. What are some of the things you "can" do in the middle of your suffering? When you do them, do they give you a sense of joy and accomplishment?

2. How will you choose to embrace the thought and practice of "Focus on what you can do, not on what you can't do"?

3. What do you believe Jesus is giving you strength for in the middle of your trial? What are you doing, with His help?

SEVENTEEN

TASTE AND SEE - THE LORD IS GOOD!

In Chapter 3, I talked about how we live our lives "after" the sudden difficulty. We live forward because time doesn't stop. However, after some time has passed, it is helpful and healthy to look back. The purpose for this is not only to see how far we've come, but mainly to see where God was with us in our difficulty.

It's good to recognize and acknowledge where God was at work in the middle of it all. Those of us who know Jesus Christ personally know that He is not far off. He is with us. He promised never to leave nor forsake us. The Holy Spirit dwells in us and He delights in showing us how He was sustaining us. Most importantly, He invites us into deeper intimacy with Him.

For a time, you may have been angry and turned away from God. Please keep this in mind: God has not turned away from you. The reality is that only God can comfort and heal our deepest pain. The Bible says He is close to the brokenhearted (Psalm 34:18).

When we are going through difficulties, I believe God desires to reveal an aspect of His character to us, one we may not yet fully appreciate or understand. As we journey deeper with Him, we come to experience and appreciate Him more. We get a broader understanding of who He is.

This has been my experience through every storm in my life. Perhaps these are the best times for God to make Himself known, because at other times we may not have been ready or as vulnerable to see His true nature. It is possible that in our pain and suffering, we become desperate enough to listen to what He has to say to us.

I'm convinced that God loves to reveal Himself to us at different times in our lives. There are so many character qualities or attributes of God. He is multi-faceted, and there's no end to who He is for us. He is Comforter, Healer, Friend, Lover, Refuge, Strength, Provider, Father, and Protector, to name a few.

In this unexpected difficulty, God became my provider in a way that He never had before. Over ten years ago, at a time when a close friend died suddenly, the Lord was my comforter. He filled me with peace and comfort during that overwhelmingly sad time, and because I experienced that, I run to Him for peace and comfort at times when I feel sorrow.

Fourteen years ago, in a time when I felt exceedingly lonely, He became my closest friend. When we know God by experience in a way we couldn't have if our difficulty hadn't happened, we gain a deep, abiding knowledge of God in that area, and we can develop an unshakeable trust in Him. I believe that so many of the trials and troubles in our lives increase our capacity to know God, then He fills that capacity, and it grows.

God delights to show up and to reveal a new part of His character to us. In the grief, shock, pain, and confusion, we may not be listening or watching and unknowingly miss what He is doing. But be assured, if we look for Him in the middle of it all, or some time after, we will see Him.

It's a worthwhile practice at times, to look back at all the difficulties in life and to consider where God was and how He showed up. While we live forward, we need to look back sometimes. It's in the looking back that we can see things more clearly.

The Israelites made a small monument on the side of the Jordan River with stones, and called them memorial stones. When people passed by that way, they told them about the miracle God did for them as they crossed into the land of Canaan (see Joshua 4:1-7).

I like to write things down in journals. That way I can go back and read what God did at a particular time in my life. When the next hard thing comes along, I have a track record of God's handiwork, care and provision.

I wonder if that's what David meant when He said, "Taste and see that the Lord is good!" (Psalm 34:8a). He was calling His fellow Israelites to look at all that God had done for them, and to remember. Our difficulties do not feel good, and we may question whether God is good as we go through them. But, when we look back, we can see where God was at work, doing things in, through, and for us in ways He never has done before.

Suffering isn't easy, especially when it comes out of nowhere and throws us off kilter. But in the looking back, and in the living today, when enough time has passed, we truly can taste and see the Lord's goodness.

God told Moses, "I am who I am" (Exodus 3:14a). This has always reminded me that God is a present tense God, not a past or future God, though He's that also. God IS, and God is with us in all that we go through. He is with us in the relatively easy seasons, and in the excruciatingly difficult ones. The question is, "Can we recognize His hand at work all around us?" In the dark moments of grief, confusion, sorrow, anger, and bewilderment, it may be hard to fully sense or acknowledge how God is at work, but trust me He is.

My story has God's fingerprints all over it. I saw His hand of care and help in the middle of what I was going through. I can clearly see these things as I look back. From the time of my accident, and for many months after, my eyes were wide open when I saw how God was taking care of tiny details, as well as big things in my life. I don't believe in luck or coincidence. There are just too many examples in my story for me not to turn to God and say "thank you" a thousand times over.

Frank Viola said it this way:

For followers of Jesus Christ, there is no such thing as coincidence. Instead, we see the fingerprints of God - which reveal His nearness and exhibit His love. Coincidence, then, is one of the ways in which the Lord speaks to us, especially when we're going through the furnace of affliction. So pay attention. [14]

Here's a list of all that I saw God doing for me.

1. On the day of my accident, my opponent on the Pickleball court was a nurse. She had been trained to handle medical emergencies. She knew exactly what to do for me, including telling me how to breathe in the shock and trauma. She remained calm, while taking charge of the situation. She was uniquely skilled to help me.

2. The surgeon had room in his schedule, or he made room, to have me come the day after my accident. It's my understanding that most surgeons have very full schedules, resulting in a waiting list.

3. Charles had no university classes the week that my

accident happened. He was able to come home to be with me when Derek had to be away on a business trip.

4. A wheelchair was available in our community within days of the surgery, giving me some mobility. Our new home in Mt. Forest had the perfect layout for this. Had the accident happened in Owen Sound, it would have been very difficult for me to navigate around my home in a wheelchair since the hallways were narrow, and it was a galley kitchen. It was a huge blessing to be able to use the wheelchair, a God-send really. It gave me some independence.

5. The local VON had time to help me. I did not have to wait, and I was the one to set the date for when they would start coming. A friend who works in healthcare was shocked when I told her that the VON was coming to my house for a few weeks, starting within a few weeks! Later, I was told that the VON do not normally see anyone younger than sixty years old, and that there is usually a wait time of months.

5. An in-home physiotherapist came right when it was time for me to start physiotherapy. This was another shock and surprise to this friend who works in healthcare. She said it was unheard of to have this service so quickly, that there's a long waiting list, and it's so unusual for a person

my age to get the service. Luck? Coincidence? I don't think so. I believe this to be the favour of God.

6. We needed to find someone to live in the empty apartment Derek was renovating. There is quite a process to advertise, review applications, and meet or interview potential tenants. For the first time, and to our great delight, the former owners had given us two applications of people who were interested six months before we even bought the building! The one person I called was still interested since he had not yet found a new place to live. On January 1, he saw the apartment while it was in the middle of the repairs; he immediately sent his last month's rent deposit, and signed a lease. He is still there today. I did not have to advertise or screen applicants other than the one.

7. We received noticed March 1, 2020 that an apartment would be vacant as of May 1. I informed the other tenants in the building that the apartment was coming available, if they knew anyone. Out of the blue, we received a call from a district manager at McDonald's. The general manager of our local McDonald's just happened to live in our apartment building, and passed on the news to her boss.

Two managers had been hired to come from overseas to work in the Hanover McDonald's; they needed a place to live for May 1, the very day the apartment would be available! I called someone who has rented to other overseas managers to verify the story because I was in disbelief. It all sounded too good to be true. Within a week, we had a signed lease, our rent deposit, and a guarantee from the owner of the McDonald's that the rent would be paid for at least one year. This is nothing short of miraculous. This had never happened to us in our many years of being landlords. Again, we did not advertise, show the apartment, or need to make a choice among different people.

In April, only weeks prior to these new tenants arriving, covid 19 was spreading worldwide, and international travel to Canada had been curtailed. I began to wonder, even worry, whether these two managers would be able to come. I wasn't sure what would happen to our signed lease, or if I would be able to get tenants in the middle of the worldwide pandemic. Many businesses were closed and people were staying home.

As I thought about these things, I knew I had to phone the owner of McDonald's to get the update. The very day I intended to make the phone call, I received a text from the tenant who works at McDonald's. The text said, "the overseas managers are not coming, but we have two employees who are being promoted to manager. They need the apartment if you are willing to rent it to them."

Immediately, I began to praise the Lord. He knows my needs before I even ask. I might have even done a happy dance. This was no coincidence. This was God's provision and favour. Those two managers stayed with us for over a year, and they were excellent tenants.

8. In July, 2020, at my seven month mark, I noticed something on my foot. It caused a lot of pain, especially when I was walking, something I was enjoying again. In August, I contacted my doctor's office. Due to the covid 19 pandemic, doctors were talking to patients via phone calls and emails. I sent a photo of my "bump". In a phone call, the nurse practitioner gave me some exercises to do, which I did. After one month, there was no change. In September, I was able to see the nurse practitioner in person who diagnosed my problem to be a ganglion cyst. Within a week, I had an ultrasound which came back with no clear results. I was booked for an MRI, which was also scheduled quickly. This yielded no clear plan. I asked to be referred to my O.R.I.F. surgeon.

I went to see my surgeon on Thursday, December 18, 2020. He confirmed that it was a ganglion cyst, and that it was sitting on the nerves of my foot. That's why I had so much pain. He gave me several choices, one of which was to have it removed, which I agreed with. Waiting for his secretary to book that surgery, I was thinking it might be February, before I could have it done. To my absolute surprise and delight, I was booked for the following Monday, December 22. Both of our sons would be home for Christmas, and both were willing to take care of the meals etc, while I recovered from my surgery. What a blessing all around!

9. In late August, 2021, eight months after my ganglion cyst was removed, I had intense pain in my foot for a couple of weeks, and mostly when I was walking. After calling the surgeon's office and pleading to have my "hardware" removed, I was called back on the same day to come in two days later. I had an x-ray, followed by an appointment with my surgeon. The surgeon was so happy with the perfect healing in my previously broken ankle, that he refused to do the surgery to remove the hardware.

Instead, he diagnosed me with plantar fasciitis, and wrote a script for physiotherapy and orthotics. I booked both appointments: shock wave therapy in his office in Guelph, and the orthotics appointment right here in Mt. Forest. After one session of shock wave therapy, armed with new exercises, and a suggestion not to wear my new running shoes, I met the foot specialist. He examined my foot, did some tests, and proceeded to tell me that everything I was doing was going to help to heal me, that I did not need the expensive custom orthotics. He didn't even charge me for the check up appointment.

After four shock wave therapy appointments, eventually walking in my new shoes, and doing the prescribed exercises, I didn't experience any pain for over two weeks when I went to Germany to accompany a close friend who was having back surgery. I walked over an hour and a half every day, and wore my shoes all day long, and enjoyed freedom from pain in that time. When I got back from Germany, I can't say that the freedom from pain has continued. I still must wear indoor shoes in and around my house and do all the stretching exercises, but I have not needed custom orthotics.

I have tasted and seen throughout my entire recovery that God was taking care of details, all kinds of details in my life. In a few cases, He took care of it before I even asked, because He knows what I need.

More significant than the progressive physical healing and the remarkable miracles of provision is what God was and is doing in my heart. I am not the same person I was when I first moved to Mt. Forest. I actually love being alone now, and I am able to relax. I don't feel the need to "do" all the time. I have never felt more secure in Christ than I do now. These are significant changes compared with all that I described myself to be in Chapter 1.

God is good regardless of whether we are physically healed or not, because His nature doesn't change. The Apostle Paul had a thorn in his flesh, which was never removed, despite him asking the Lord to remove it on three occasions. He resolved himself to the fact that God's grace is sufficient, and that God's strength is made perfect in our weakness (2 Corinthians 12:7b-9). The Lord is good and He is always at work. That's a truth worth remembering.

I believe that the benefit of a heart change in trials far outweighs the benefit of physical healing.

QUESTIONS:

1. What do you think about the examples Wendy gave? Do you agree that it was the Lord providing for her needs or would you be more likely to call them coincidences?

2. In your times of struggle and suffering, describe the ways in which you have seen God at work behind the scenes?

3. Thinking back on the difficulties in your life, what aspects of God's character are you absolutely convinced of; what have you experienced first-hand?

EIGHTEEN

SILENCE IS GOLDEN

As I detailed in Chapter 1, my life before moving to Mt. Forest was busy. Then we moved, Charles left for university, and my life got un-busy. Very un-busy. Then on one day, everything stopped. I went from tons of activity, to some activity, to absolutely no activity, and add to that...silence. Deafening silence. Clock ticking silence.

Derek worked at his job, then worked on our renovation at the apartment building. He was gone six days a week from 9am to 6:30pm. My house was silent and I was completely alone, apart from my dog. I had no human company for ten hours a day, day after day after day. If the change in my lifestyle after moving wasn't enough, add the shock and pain from the broken ankle and surgery, plus the silence and aloneness. It was challenging to handle all of this at the same time.

Yet, as I type these words now, I am sitting in silence and alone. Derek is away at a work event, and I am loving it! One of the biggest changes that came from my season of silence was that I now find I need and enjoy silence, quiet, and aloneness. It is in silence and in being alone that I think best, write best, and hear the voice of the Lord the best.

Before, I hated silence. I filled it with background music or I had to be with people. I filled my days with people. But it was in the silence, in the days and weeks after my accident, that I came to realize that I was addicted to people, busy-ness, noise, and activity.

Being forced into a season of rest, stillness, and non-activity was the most life changing experience I have ever walked through, and now I yearn for quiet in my days. I am finding that being around a lot of people and activity exhausts me, whereas before, it energized me. I find that I am completely out of sorts now if I don't have some silence or quiet in my days. That's quite a turn-around!

Each hard season we encounter can be transformative IF we take the time to ask the Lord what He wants us to do in the season in which we find ourselves. We can't assume anything. Doing what we did before won't yield the new fruit that God is developing. It's worth waiting on the Lord to discover the new thing in the abrupt change of the rhythm of life.

For me, it was all about rest, not initiating texts with

people, allowing Him to bring exactly what and who I needed when I needed it. Even though my flesh was screaming for things I wanted, I came to recognize that those things weren't the best things for me in that time. This is very difficult; it requires self-control and surrender, but I declare with certainty, that it is well worth it!

I could have easily drowned out the silence with podcasts, worship music, Netflix, phone conversations, YouTube videos and the like, but instead, I drowned out the noise of life with silence.

I sat on my couch looking out the window as the snow fell gently to the ground. I noticed when my neighbours came and went to work. I saw the day my neighbour moved in two doors down from me; she has now become a close friend. I watched the sunrise through the trees, and I watched people walk by. I was able to watch a robin building her nest, the eggs being laid, the baby birds being born, and them eventually leaving the nest. This was wonderful, something I looked forward to each day, and it was all from the view of our bathroom window.

I might not have noticed these things before had my life taken on the busyness I was accustomed to. I journaled page after page of prayers, and emotions, including the good, bad and ugly, as well as the conversations I had with the Lord. I read the Bible a lot, writing down "endurance" and affirmation Scriptures. I also devoured many Christian fiction books on my phone via Google Play Books, as well as other books we had unpacked when we first moved in. Within a month of my accident, I started doing diamond art, again often in the silence, though sometimes with worship music.

Sitting alone in that season after a lifetime of busy activity, was exactly what I needed, though I did not want it. As I write these words, currently sitting in silence, I can hear a clock ticking, a dog barking in the distance, and I feel an overwhelming sense of calm and peace. I feel the Lord's presence with me. This has been such a profound change.

The prophet Isaiah said, "In quietness and trust is your strength" (Isaiah 30:15b), which is so counter cultural. It is opposed to everything I had learned. I'm so pleased to say that I did gain trust and strength in the Lord through that season of silence, through being very alone for the first time in my life.

It was also incredibly lonely. I often cried out to the Lord for my friends or anyone to come and visit me, for someone to see me in my pain. But God saw me. In His presence I was comforted. In His presence, my flesh was quieted.

"Trials teach us what we are; they dig up the soil, and let us see what we are made of."
Charles Spurgeon

Pressing into silence, solitude and inactivity is a good way to get a handle on what all is going on inside of us. Though it's not the most enjoyable experience, we really do need to know what we are thinking and feeling. As we wait on the Lord, we will get an idea of what it is He's trying to show us. This isn't something that happens immediately. It takes time. As C. S. Lewis said:

"God whispers to us in our pleasures, speaks in our conscience, but shouts in our pain: it is His megaphone to rouse a deaf world."

Let's allow God to shout to us in our pain, and let's get quiet enough to hear Him. He has something to say to us at this time. For it is at this time in our lives that we might be surrendered or vulnerable enough to accept it! In times of suffering, if we get alone long enough, our thoughts can get very loud, and we can see who we really are.

I wrote this thoughts in my journal - the Lord did show me some things about myself:

You know me inside and out. I give you permission to reveal me to me - so that I can change to be more like you.
(Journal, January 13, 2020)

I discovered that I was living with an attitude of entitlement around my health. I also came to terms with the reality that I was incredibly dependent on people. I looked back over my life and saw that in many situations, when I was struggling, I turned to people for comfort, answers, and company, rather than running to Jesus Christ. I had so many idols and false gods in my life, and many of these were exposed in my times of silence. This gave me the opportunity to see them, confess them, and ask the Lord for help in turning away from them.

In the quiet, and especially now that I look back, I also see that I did have a strong faith and trust in the Lord. I had to admit that I had a wrong understanding of the sovereignty of God, and of my role as His daughter. He was helping me to see myself and my wrong thinking and attitudes. He was bringing me into a place of truth - an unencumbered walk of truth.

After all, Jesus said, "the truth will set you free" (John 8:32). Jesus is The Truth, and He desires us to be free to walk with Him, to look to Him for help in times of trouble, and to grow in trust in Him. This faith test, which James says is designed to produce perseverance, was demonstrating to me that I had been maturing in my faith and endurance. But I still had a ways to go! I'm so happy that these trials don't only expose areas of weakness, but they also illuminate some of our new and growing strengths.

Psalm 46:10 says, "Be still and know that I am God". I was being still physically, but inside my soul, I was restless, impatient, and anxious. I was demanding healing and a speedy recovery. I was making assumptions and presumptions about the Lord, and about the process I was in.

That is, until I surrendered, which certainly took some time. It was a process, and it needed to happen. I am not God. So, at a point in my journey of recovery from the sudden suffering, I needed to get out of the way of myself, and let the God of the Bible, the one who created the heavens and the earth, have His way. He is sovereign. He is doing the work. His goal is to make me more like Christ.

My job is simply to trust Him in the process and to worship Him for He is worthy. Who was I to demand certain things from God? He is the potter and I am the clay. He was doing something that I couldn't understand in the heat of the moment, in the depth of the pain, but I could trust that He was at work. The Bible says He is, and I have seen the amazing things He's done in the past.

Here are two journal entries that illustrate how I began to take hold of some truth, and that the change was beginning to take hold in me:

Lord, thank you, thank you, thank you. I'm learning to enjoy being alone, being my own friend, not needing the company, or affirmation, sympathy and coddling of others – I trust you, Holy Spirit, to bring who and what is needed, when it is needed. You know my needs – and I need a lot less than I

thought. I love the simple life, Lord God.
(January, January 5, 2020)

So very thankful to be alone – in the quiet stillness.
Oh Lord, I'll never be the same. I crave the hush. I love the
quiet – hush – I can think. I can hear you.
(Journal, January 20, 2020)

As John 15 describes, I am the branch, Jesus is the vine, and the Father is the vinedresser. I was being pruned! If you've ever pruned a rose bush, it looks ghastly afterwards, ugly and small. But the next season it is large and full of beautiful blooms. More fruit! That's the goal behind the pruning seasons of our lives. However, in the middle of it, when all we see and feel is what has been lopped off, all we often feel is the hurt of the loss. We feel naked, bare, vulnerable, and weak.

Weakness is a feeling and a state of being that this world condemns. It's certainly something I didn't like feeling. The truth is, however, if we never admit our weaknesses, then God's strength cannot be demonstrated in our lives. The Lord said to the Apostle Paul: "My grace is sufficient for you, for my power is made perfect in weakness" (2 Corinthians 12:9a). Paul wrote this while he was in prison, and while he was plagued with "a thorn in the flesh" that the Lord did not remove.

God is good, and He desires your good. What we walk

through at times is so incredibly painful, hard, seemingly unfair, yet in the middle of it all, God is still good. He is still sovereign. He is up to something, and we can taste and see Him in the middle of it. But we have got to get quiet enough to let Him speak.

It is helpful to shut out the noise and busy-ness around us long enough or consistently enough to seek the Lord and ask, "What do you want me to know?" Though we might not love the message we receive, we can trust the messenger. We can trust that He loves us enough to help us to become who He has fashioned us to be. Through our hardships and sufferings, He is the One who can help us to change the most.

I was a captive audience on that couch of mine. I had nowhere to go, no plans to make, and no distractions. I chose not to distract myself. Each one of us can do that.

QUESTIONS:

1. What is your attitude towards silence, aloneness, and inactivity? Do you agree that it is the place where you can hear the voice of the Lord the most clearly? Have you ever tried to shut out the noise and distractions around you to intentionally hear from God?

2. Have you ever been pruned by the Lord? What did it look and feel like? Have you experienced the "more fruit" that is promised afterwards? Have you surrendered to allow God to work in and through you, to change you to be more like Him?

3. St. Augustine is quoted as saying, "Our hearts are restless until they rest in you", referring to resting in Jesus Christ. Where are you at in that process? Is your heart and soul at rest in Christ? If not, why do you think that is? How can you come to that place of rest and peace?

NINETEEN

NORMAL HAS SHIFTED

This journey is oh so hard, and honestly it's lonely. I'm not sure how much to push and when to back off. I'm tired a lot. And I think that's normal, but it's not my normal. So Lord, is normal gone for me? – perhaps there's a new normal – it's all about trusting God.

(Journal, Feb 10, 2020)

Two steps forward and one step backward. That's the way it is with recovery at times. In fact, that's what the VON PSW told me many times in the first four weeks after my surgery. I can say that I fully expected that at the three year mark, I wouldn't still need to do daily exercises. But I do. Most days, I must do various exercises before putting my feet on the floor in the morning. I didn't think I would be suffering with joint pain when the seasons change or the barometric pressure fluctuates. But alas I am.

Each season of suffering can leave residual physical pain and negative feelings or thoughts for some time, perhaps not every day, but certainly some days. The trauma and change to our lives from unexpected events can leave us flabbergasted and asking "what just happened?". It can take far more time to regain equilibrium than we fully comprehend.

The statements "It takes as long as it takes. Be gentle on yourself.", and "we live forward, even though we wish we could live in the time before everything changed" are true statements to remind ourselves. The reality is that these lessons take time to really sink in, and then to live them out.

I mentioned in an earlier chapter, that I am or have been okay with the fact that my foot isn't the same as it was before my shattering - and it won't be, because I now have hardware. I stated that even though there has been pain, loneliness, and heartache, there has also been tremendous blessings, spiritual growth, new hobbies, a clearer understanding of chronic pain and suffering, and amazing provision from the Lord. I believe all of that. I am thankful for the circumstance that rendered me immobile for a time, a time when nearly every support I had wasn't there.

Without this sudden suffering, I don't think God could have done the surgery on my heart and mind that

He did. I don't think I would have come to understand my unhealthy dependence on people without the removal of all my props.

I say that, and I say this: about nine months ago, as my ankle was in pain and stiffness, these words popped out of my mouth, "Oh, I just wish my ankle was normal again!" I said those words with my husband standing nearby. His response? "Well, it won't be normal again." That was another "it is what it is" moment, and yet I yearn and long at times not to have to experience the pain, stiffness, and irritation associated with an ankle that broke, had a ganglion cyst grow and be removed, and then developed plantar fasciitis.

It was a time to surrender once again. It was yet another humbling moment, a reminder to lean on the Lord, and a realization that I still haven't fully embraced my new reality. I suspect this need to surrender will be an on-going posture for me for many months to come! It really does take time to accept the truth about our "new normal".

The normal we knew prior to our sudden suffering has shifted. It is no more. Things will not be the same or go back to exactly the way they were before "the thing" happened. A season of sudden suffering has a way of catapulting us into something so unfamiliar that it feels abnormal. It feels disconcerting.

We don't know how to live, think, or be in this new life. It's a good thing that God hasn't moved. Jesus is still with us. The Holy Spirit is still our counselor, comforter and friend. God is still sovereign. Though our entire world may have shifted, and our normal is no more, God is still exactly where He is and always has been.

My normal these days? I wake up and don't get out of bed right away. I do about twenty foot rotations, spell the alphabet by moving my foot and ankle this way and that, stretch and massage my foot before I put my feet on the floor. Then I must immediately put my feet into indoor shoes. Then, if necessary, I do some calf stretches, and go up and down on the toes of my left foot. I don't wear funky boots, high heels, or flats, and I can't walk around in bare feet very long or I will experience pain. I don't take my indoor shoes off except to take a shower, or put on my shoes to go outside.

As I write these things, I am sad. Recently, I watched a few younger women come into our church service with these really great boots. I have a pair in my closet too, but I can't wear them anymore. They aren't going to help my foot since they will only cause me pain. It's solid running or functional shoes for me from now on.

This is a new thing I have to get used to, and a thing I can choose to complain about or embrace as the changed normal. It is a choice. All of the changes from what was so called "normal" take time to adjust to. It takes a lot of rethinking, a lot of laying down of expectations.

Will normal come back? No. Normal has shifted! Will

I be able to go back to other types of shoes? I don't know. But right now, in the present, I cannot. I have to be extra aware of what I am wearing on my feet and how much support there is under the arch etc.

Yet, and here's the blessing part, I can wear skates, and during the winter of 2021/2022, I skated three times a week, up to fifty minutes each time, without experiencing pain or discomfort! I can wear winter boots, even walking upwards of fifty minutes in them. I can shake, dance, and boogie to music at home - when no one is watching. I can stand on my feet for longer periods of time, which means some of what I considered normal has come back.

What's next? I don't know, but there are other things I used to do that I don't do anymore. That normal has shifted too. I am learning to fully embrace those things too.

I love my new quiet life Lord. It's so weird. Some trauma and pain, and complete change was what I needed to really slow down enough to hear you clearly – I really enjoy the quiet, the slow pace – and the process of self discovery, intimacy and understanding reality.

(Journal, January 7, 2020)

It's not all bad. For the first time in my fifty seven years, I have begun to enjoy being alone with myself. I don't need to be in constant contact with others. That's a good thing - a new thing I never expected, but I am so glad it has happened. That's just one. There are others.

Over time, we can be amazed at the new things we've learned. Some of these new things may be things we never would have considered or thought we were capable of doing, let alone enjoying.

As I have said in previous chapters, when we hang onto our relationship with Christ, rehearsing Scripture, giving thanks daily, and living in the present reality, we are propelled into thoughts and places we wouldn't have imagined before. I can only speak from my own experience and story.

I now think that normal is over rated. God doesn't want us to live in normal all the time. We are called to abundant living, to joyful living, to surrendered living. Isaiah 43:19 says, "Behold, I am doing a new thing; now it springs forth, do you not perceive it? I will make a way in the wilderness and rivers in the desert."

The Apostle Paul wrote, in Philippians 1:6, "And I am sure of this, that he who began a good work in you will bring it to completion at the day of Jesus Christ". He also proclaimed, "But one thing I do: forgetting what lies behind and straining forward to what lies ahead, I press on toward the goal for the prize of the upward call of God in Christ Jesus" (Philippians 3:13b-15).

These things are beginning to make more sense to me now that quite a bit of time has passed from the original trauma. Even reading through my notes from a study I did over two years ago, I can see I no longer struggle in some of the areas I did. Jesus has given me the victory.

Even sitting here today writing this book, I can see that God is doing a new thing. I don't want normal anymore. I want an abnormal life. I desire an Ephesians 3:20 lifestyle - "Now to him who is able to do far more abundantly than all that we ask or think, according to the power at work within us." The main reason I desire this is so that others ask questions, and I can point them to Jesus Christ.

The early disciples turned the world upside down by their abnormal lives. They lived in severe persecution and still evangelized everyone around them. They helped each other, lived in joy, sang in prison, were beaten for their faith, and forgave those who did the beating. Their response to their suffering was completely abnormal. People took notice. They asked questions. That's the kind of abnormal I hope for.

Our suffering is not the end of the story, but rather the beginning of a huge story that God is writing for us, one in which, even in our suffering, we glorify Him, experience Him, declare His goodness, and proclaim thanksgiving.

Normal shifts every time we experience suffering or change, and the new season allows God to reveal Himself to us in a whole new way.

Thank you for shifting me. It took a massive injury and weeks/months on my butt to work this change in me and old

habits out of me. I'm still a work in progress, that's for sure.
(Journal, February 19, 2020)

I know I sound abnormal to say that normal is over rated as no one would wish for suffering. Suffering hurts so much; it's excruciating at times. That's true, and I agree wholeheartedly. I hate suffering and yet in my suffering, I experienced transformation, and I know it could not have happened any other way.

Our response in the midst of suffering says something to a watching world. It should be different, so "not normal", that others want to know what we have that they don't.

QUESTIONS:

1. What do you think about Wendy's statement that "normal has shifted", and that trials mean the normal you knew is no more?

2. Are you longing to live an abnormal life - one full of joy, peace, and patience - in times of suffering? Or do you hope to escape the trials of this life? Be honest.

3. What do your words and actions during suffering say to the world around you? What do you think you'll need in order to suffer with a good attitude?

TWENTY

CRUSHING CREATES A BETTER YOU

"A gem cannot be polished without friction, nor a man perfected without trials." [15]

We all have a choice when suffering, sorrow, pain, and sickness overthrows our equilibrium and shakes us to the very core. At some point along our journey, we need to ask ourselves this question:

"Do I want to be better or bitter?"

Trust me, this question is most definitely one we all must come to terms with, and we all have a choice. In the shock, trauma, pain and abruptness of the suffering, this may not enter our sphere of thinking, but when some time has passed, and we come out the other side, it is worth considering. Do

I want to be better or bitter? Here are my thoughts on this eight months after my surgery:

A person who lives with pain/suffering can grow so close to the Lord or they can grow cold and bitter.
(Journal, August 12, 2020)

To be bitter is to rehearse the unfairness of the situation. It involves turning away from God, perhaps even shaking a fist at God, or giving over to the negative feelings. It can mean staying stuck in the past, longing for things to go back to the way they were before "this" happened. We might choose to blame anyone and everyone, including God, for what we are going through.

We've all been there at some point or another in our lives. Life can be brutally hard and things can completely blind side us, even shatter us to the ground. However, focusing on oneself can cause us to remain in bitterness, which is incredibly harmful - emotionally, mentally and physically.

On the other hand, releasing our anger, sorrow, and what may even be the start of bitterness is a process. I strongly recommend this. It's not easy to do, but it is worth it. Surrendering to the sovereignty of God is actually freeing in so many ways. We no longer have to make things happen, or think that we are responsible for our own healing or recovery.

We simply need to live in the moments, day by day, enjoying what we've been given, no matter how small it may seem. Perhaps seeing the sun rise and getting out of bed is one thing to embrace. Having a mind set on Jesus Christ grants us possibilities and opportunities that bring health and hope, and all of these things will help us endure our suffering season.

I agree whole-heartedly with these words from Frank Viola's book *Hang On, Let Go*.

"The crucible of adversity is meant to radically transform your life." [16]

It is really hard for me to fully explain the many ways in which I am no longer the same person after experiencing my painful, lonely, confusing season where I was immobile, followed by ongoing physical pain and weakness. It was not at all what I had expected my life to look like, but it did happen.

As I've shared through the pages of this book, God's hand was there and I can see His fingerprints all over my story. The change is so profound within me, so much more than the physical recovery of my ankle, that today I really don't even recognize the person I was when I first moved to Mt. Forest three months prior to my accident.

Because I pressed into the Lord, encouraged myself in Him, practiced gratitude, looked for where He was at work, embraced new ways of living, and learned to get creative with how to live with some pain and limitation, I know I am better. I am not bitter. This is also possible for anyone after a shattering experience. At one point, I wrote these words:

I've learned a few things about myself – I've been a spoiled brat. I've been upset at not getting my own way. This difficulty has truly been good. I'm growing up. Gratitude is growing. It's okay to be sad, to grieve, to be frustrated; and I can use my energy for good: not wallowing, but pushing myself. While I would have liked a lot more attention from people, it's not what I needed. Joy, peace, and genuine contentment are inner works – no human can help me feel those things. It's only in relationship with Christ that these things come.

(Journal, December 20, 2019)

I feel like I'm on the potter's wheel being re-made – new thoughts, new priorities, new relationships. It's all very strange and yet I know that God is the author of it. My job? Yield. Surrender. Don't complain. Choose a good attitude. I feel as though relationships, friendships, and my comfort zone is being stripped and I don't know what the future looks like.

(Journal, December 31, 2019)

It was through this season of sudden suffering, where I felt crushed to the core, broken physically and emotionally, that I began to actually relate to so many of the Scriptures about suffering. My life had been pretty sheltered and sweet up to the point of my sudden suffering. There had been some difficult times, like when close friends die. I've also experienced betrayal that came out of nowhere. I've been slandered, maligned, and gossiped about. I've been deeply lonely at having moved to new communities with no friends.

This time there was something so much deeper when I found myself alone for hours and hours while immobilized because of my broken ankle. I was knocked down so severely that it shook my whole belief system about my life. I'm not exactly sure why, but this was a significantly deeper level of suffering.

Maybe it's because I never saw it coming. It broke apart all my assumptions about my life. It also shattered every wrong presumption I had about God and His healing power. I assumed things and didn't understand the deeper work He was after. I didn't comprehend why I needed to learn to persevere, and that it was going to take some time.

The Apostle Paul wrote,

Not only that, but we rejoice in our sufferings, knowing that suffering produces endurance, and endurance produces character, and character produces hope, and hope does not put us to shame, because God's love has been poured out into our hearts through the Holy Spirit, who has been given to us. (Romans 5:3-5).

This is what I wrote in my journal:

Some, maybe all trials or troubles have to be worked out alone with the Lord to get their full benefit. Perseverance leads to maturity. It's up to me how I use this time, how I ask for help, how I learn to manage on my own. You are with me. People cannot do or give what you do. I am at your mercy O God – you have complete control of my life. I have no control. I release my wrong thoughts, my impatience, and immaturity to you, and I surrender again O God.

(Journal, December 20, 2020)

There clearly has never been a time in the past where God could have had my undivided attention as He had during those months I was alone. I feel privileged to have been chosen to suffer in that way, because I truly can say I will never be the same, and I'm so thankful for that.

The way I relate to my friends and family is very different. I now give them freedom to be themselves, rather than placing expectations on them. I enjoy new interests and spend time at activities that I had previously thought were frivolous - like painting and writing. It is in these activities that my mind, though active, feels the most at rest with my life and my Lord.

Here's how I expressed these thoughts in my journal:

I believe thankfulness and contentment is one of my new mindsets. I really don't think I had it before. I am pleased and thankful for your trusting in me, your care and concern for me, that you would take me through this narrow gate to squeeze more of my flesh out – that I would become more like you O God.

(Journal January 10, 2020)

There can be great joy in the journey when our minds and hearts are fixed on the truth that God is with us, that He will never leave, and that He has a purpose for our pain and suffering. It's a good thing that Jesus warned His disciples, and us, that "in the world you will have tribulation" (John 16:33), and Peter said "do not be surprised at the fiery trial" (1 Peter 4:12), and James said, "count it all joy when you meet trials of various kinds" (James 1:3a). We need these reminders.

We aren't alone in our suffering. There is a cloud of witnesses cheering us on to "finish well". Let's not give up what the Lord could be working in us. Let's not take the road of complaint or bitterness. Let's take the road that leads to peace with Jesus. Let's surrender, yield, and recognize that our God who is good is also sovereign. He knows what He is doing.

Kelly Minter describes it well:

It's along the journey where our faith and endurance are refined. Sometimes I interpreted those experiences (hard times) as God's punishment or condemnation. Later, I realized it was just the opposite. He was using that space to do more than I could have hoped, beyond what my finite imagination could have dreamt. The treasures He wanted me to find along the way couldn't have been found elsewhere, and I couldn't have known the greatest prize - deep intimacy with Christ - any other way. [17]

The question remains, "do you want to be better or bitter?" The recovery process can be long; it can be hard; and it can include many twists and turns. But, if we hang on tightly to our Saviour, He will work all things together for good. He will transform us from glory to ever increasing glory, into Christ-likeness. He will continue the thing He started, and we will be blessed beyond measure. We will not be the same after our sudden suffering: we can't be. But we can be better, beyond what we ever thought or imagined possible.

This journal entry expresses my heart and surrender:

This furnace of affliction truly is refining me; it's a purifying place. I never really understood how immature I was until I suffered physical loss and pain. This was so needed Lord. Truly. And thank you for not healing me instantly. I don't know if I would have just gone back to old behaviours and patterns.

(Journal, May 27, 2020)

Let's press into whatever Christ has for us, wherever He is leading. Let's learn to trust His transformation process.

QUESTIONS:

1. In your crushing, refining, and pruning times, how has God changed you from the inside out? Can you name the things He revealed to you about yourself, and about Himself?

2. Have you become better or bitter in your suffering seasons? What seasons do you find harder than others? If you recognize bitterness in your life right now, will you choose to work through it so that you can become better?

3. Where are you seeing transformation in your life? How is God changing you from glory to glory?

TWENTY ONE

THE LORD IS MY SHEPHERD

The Lord is my shepherd; I shall not want. He makes me lie down in green pastures. He leads me beside still waters. He restores my soul. He leads me in paths of righteousness for his name's sake. Even though I walk through the valley of the shadow of death, I will fear no evil, for you are with me; your rod and your staff, they comfort me. You prepare a table before me in the presence of my enemies; you anoint my head with oil; my cup overflows. Surely goodness and mercy shall follow me all the days of my life, and I shall dwell in the house of the Lord forever. (Psalm 23)

If there is anything I learned along my journey of sudden suffering, it's that I did not truly believe or live out the "I shall not want" part of Psalm 23:1. The Holman Christian Standard Bible says, "There is nothing I lack." Reading back through the previous chapters, I can see that I read and wrote out Psalm 23. I have outlined the concept of walking through the valley, that the Lord was with me. I illustrated how He provided everything I needed. But the reality is this: He did not provide everything I wanted.

With a sudden halt to all activity in my life, I suddenly felt like I lacked many good things. During my time of being stripped of everything familiar, being in physical pain, shock, and confusion, with hours alone for the first time in my life, I wanted a lot of things.

I wanted relief from the pain and suffering, so much so that I proclaimed, declared, prayed and expected the Lord to give me instant and miraculous healing. I wanted to avoid the trial. My preconceived notion of what my life was supposed to look like suddenly was no longer a reality. Talk about my bubble bursting. I did not like or want that. I wanted people to come to me, to comfort me, to sit on my ash pile as Job's friends did.

As I think about it now, I see that I did have some friends who did as Job's friends did - they tried to explain the "why" behind my suffering. Unfortunately, this didn't help me in my estimation of the sovereign Lord. I wanted my life to be normal again, as if the accident had never happened.

The upheaval in my life was profound and abrupt, and it was exactly what I needed in order to learn that Jesus Christ really is enough. Here's my journal entry about this:

You supplied what I needed when I needed it, not my wants, whines or complaints. I am coming to trust you all the more, dear Lord. You are so good to me and I am pleased to spend this time alone with you. I don't need people to fill me – they are a wonderful bonus and a blessing. You fill me. You complete me. You are sufficient.

(Journal, January 10, 2020)

I can see now that had I been granted miraculous healing, I would have missed all of the transformation that has happened in my thinking, emotions, and understanding of who God is and who I am.

I would not have learned how to depend on Him alone. I would not have understood just how dependent I had been on people or how proud and self-sufficient I was. I would not have recognized that I leaned on my own understanding a lot. I would not have realized how immature and entitled I was. I know I wouldn't have come to a deeper understanding of the value, beauty and purpose of suffering with Christ had I not experienced the season of sudden suffering. I would have missed out on all that God had planned for me to become more Christ-like.

If you are a Christian, it is His intent to transform you into Christ's image. He knows just how to do that, and often it is in the hard places that the most change will happen. I declared this in the following journal entry:

Thank you for how you're showing me that I have everything I need. Right here. I have nothing to complain about. I accept what is and believe that you are good.

(Journal, December 15, 2019)

I am so thankful that the Lord knew what I needed, and He provided. He truly is enough, not just materially, but emotionally and relationally, too. He alone satisfies the deep longings of our hearts, and He knows how to comfort us far better than any human can. It is important to receive help, to reach out for help in our times of suffering, but to rely too much on people isn't a good thing. I certainly enjoyed the company of many people in my recovery, but the company of Jesus Christ truly surpassed them all.

The Lord truly does want to be our present help in times of trouble. He wants to be the friend that sticks closer than the brother. He desires to be our Comforter, Counselor, Everlasting Father and Prince of Peace. He is Lord, and He knows what He is doing! I started to realize this:

The biggest thing about this situation? Admitting and acknowledging that I have limitations, and that I can't do what I want, when I want. And yet, Lord, you just keep showing up, showing me you're with me and that it's all okay.

(Journal, April 15, 2020)

Recently, I completed a Bible study on Psalm 23, in which many references were made to Phillip Keller's book, *A Shepherd Looks at Psalm 23*. Being a shepherd himself, he gives a unique perspective on each verse of Psalm 23, including examples about his own sheep, the landscape and sheep rearing practices of ancient Israel, and the nature of human beings, which the Bible describes as sheep (God's Words, not mine!).

Keller says, "...it is no mere whim on God's part to call us sheep. Our behavior patterns and life habits are so much like that of sheep it is well nigh embarrassing". [18]

The intimate care and concern the shepherd has for his sheep is but a minuscule representation of how deeply our Good Shepherd, Jesus Christ cares for us, His sheep. In reading Keller's book, I found a few things worth noting:

...His (Jesus Christ's) ownership of me as a human being is legitimate simply because it is He who brought me into being and no one is better able to understand or care for me. [19]

I shall not want...the sentiment of a sheep utterly satisfied with its owner, perfectly content with its lot in life. ... being utterly contented in the Good Shepherd's care and consequently not craving or desiring anything more. [20]

A flock that is restless, discontented, always agitated and disturbed never does well. And the same is true of people.....

nothing so quieted and reassured the sheep as to see me in the field. There is nothing like Christ's presence to dispel the fear, the panic, the terror of the unknown. [21]

The disappointments, the frustrations, the discouragements, the dilemmas, the dark, difficult days, though they be shadowed valleys need not be disasters. They can be the road to higher ground in our walk with God. [22]

I'm so glad that I have come to a place of deeper understanding of this nature of God, the Good Shepherd, and that He promises to be with us as we go through valleys, trials, difficulties, and suffering.

One more journal entry:

I know I have a whole new theology on suffering and I'm so glad for it. It's not about removal, rescue, escape out of trials – it's about being transformed through them. I walk THROUGH the valley of the shadow of death. There are valleys, but You are with us. We don't need to fear. I truly am pleased and amazed at the work and change you wrought.

(Journal, October 9, 2021)

QUESTIONS:

1. Have the trials and sufferings you've encountered led you to an understanding of the Lord as your Good Shepherd? If not, why do you think that is?

2. How have you experienced the nearness of God when you've walked through your dark valleys (seasons)?

3. Wendy has said that the Lord gave her what she needed, but not always what she wanted. What do you think about that? Do you trust that God knows what you need?

FINAL THOUGHTS

Well, there you have it! Thus concludes this chapter in my story, a story of a particular season in time when God met me, sustained me, provided and cared for me, revealing His goodness and mercy in ways He likely couldn't have done so at any other time.

I was captive to Him, His voice, His kindness, and His sufficiency. I'm so glad that He didn't simply bring about my physical healing. Oh no! He was after much more than that. He was after restoring my soul.

Praying away pain, trials, waiting aborts what the Lord could do in that time. Refining: it's critical to maturity. It doesn't feel good at all but to grow up and really trust God? It's necessary.
(Journal, March 8, 2021)

As strange as it sounds, I'm glad it's taken a long time and that it's not over yet - I have more lessons to learn. Why? Because in no other season of my life have I experienced so much transformation in my thoughts, attitudes, priorities, and in my understanding about the Lord God, or about my own presumptions, expectations and flawed theology. I'm so thankful for the women who journeyed with me, who encouraged me, and brought truth when I needed to hear it.

This season of deep pain and loneliness was the greatest catalyst to intimacy with Jesus Christ and with my husband. I am so thankful for his faithful Job-like patience as he took the brunt of so many of my emotions and confusion. We are in a totally new place and it's been absolutely marvelous. As I said, when one experiences a drastic event in their lives, it can't not affect the people around them.

Thank you for journeying with me. I hope that there are some nuggets that you will be able to take away with you on your journey, and most especially when you are struck with a season of sudden suffering. Before I finish this book, I wanted to leave a few parting thoughts. As it were, the crux of the matter:

"We must come to terms with a sovereign God during our adversity or we'll never understand or respond to our sufferings correctly." [23]

After reading those words by Frank Viola, this is what I wrote in my journal:

I read that recently. WOW. That would have to be one of the greatest lessons I have learned. God is sovereign. He does what He pleases and He owes no one an explanation. Oh, Father, thank you that you know all things - and all things work for your purposes, which are good.

(Journal entry, February 12, 2022)

King Solomon wrote twelve long chapters in the book of Ecclesiastes. His summary conclusion near the end of his life was:

"Let us hear the conclusion of the whole matter: Fear God and keep His commandments, For this is man's all" (Ecclesiastes 12:13, NKJV).

In the middle of what one might consider the worst suffering any human in the Bible underwent, apart from Jesus Christ, Job said, "Though He slay me, yet will I trust Him" (Job 13:15a, NKJV).

Lastly, the prophet Habakkuk had this to say in the middle of the coming destruction and invasion by the Babylonians. It is part of a long prayer but these are the concluding verses:

"Though the fig tree should not blossom,
Nor fruit be on the vines,
The produce of the olive fail
And the fields yield no food,
The flock be cut off from the fold,
And there be no herd in the stalls,
Yet I will rejoice in the LORD;
I will take joy in the God of my salvation.
God, the Lord is my strength;
He makes my feet like the deer's;
He makes me tread on my high places."
(Habakkuk 3:17-19)

I am convinced that we can and we must remember who our God is in the middle of our suffering, as these biblical giants exemplified. God is sovereign. He will bring good out of our suffering. It is possible to worship Him in the middle of our difficulties. It is possible, sometimes best when looking back, to see what God is or has been up to.

It is possible to raise an Ebenezer (memorial stone) and tell others what God has done in the middle and after our seasons of suffering. "We should delight to describe, in detail, the hard experiences through which He has brought us." [24]

If you are a believer in Christ, He can do for you all that He has done for me, and more, if you but keep your eyes on Him, your ears open to Him, and the fire of your faith burning, even flickering. It's been a real blessing and honour to be able to share my story with you. If you have come through a suffering season and God has met you and sustained you, tell others. Testimonies are powerful. They are how we overcome (Revelation 12:11).

If you do not know the God I have been speaking about, you can. He is know-able. He is alive. He is the One true God. He has revealed Himself in the pages of the Holy Bible.

If you want to discover Him, start reading the book of John. I recommend the English Standard Version (ESV). The gospel of John reveals Jesus Christ, our Saviour, who came to the earth over two thousand years ago, to be Immanuel, God with us. He lived a perfect, sinless life - something not one of us can do. He died, paying the penalty for our sins.

Our sins have caused us to be totally separated from God who is the source of all life. When Jesus rose, defeating death, He made a way for us to be reconciled to God. All who have faith to believe He is who He says He is, will experience His peace and presence, enjoy a relationship with Him as Lord and Saviour, and will live forever with Him in heaven.

I can't imagine my life without Him!

1. www.Healthline.com/health/orif-surgery

2. www.helpguide.org

3. www.healthline.com, written by Kimberly Holland, updated on September 25, 2018

4. Frank Viola, Hang On Let Go, (Carol Stream: Tyndale, 2021), 135

5. Brent Curtis and John Eldredge, The Sacred Romance, (Nashville: Thomas Nelson, 1997), 147

6. https://www.forbes.com/sites/amymorin/2014/11/23/7 -scientifically-proven-benefits-of-gratitude-that-will-motivate-you-to-give-thanks-year-round)

7. Dr Caroline Leaf FaceBook page November 26, 2000, 5 Scientific Benefits of Gratitude

8. Mark Buchanan, Your God is too safe, (Grand Rapids: Multnomah, 2001), 93

9. https://www.blueletterbible.org/lexicon/g2675/nasb20/tr/0-1/

10. https://www.blueletterbible.org/lexicon/g4741/nasb20/tr/0-1/

11. https://www.blueletterbible.org/lexicon/g4599/nasb20/tr/0-1/

12. https://www.blueletterbible.org/lexicon/g2311/nasb20/tr/0-1/

13. Kelly Minter, No Other gods, (Nashville: Lifeway Press, 2017), 90

14. Viola, 53

15. https://www.quotespedia.org/authors/l/lucius-annaeus-seneca/a-gem-cannot-be-polished-without-friction-nor-a-man-perfected-without-trials-lucius-annaeus-seneca/

16. Viola, 56

17. Minter, 163

18. Phillip Keller, A Shepherd Looks at Psalm 23, (Grand Rapids: Zondervan, 1970), 74

19. Keller, 19

20. Keller, 26

21. Keller, 36-37

22. Keller, 129

23. Viola, 326

24. Keller, 138

ACKNOWLEDGMENTS

When I started writing this book, I had no idea how much time, effort, energy and endurance would be needed! Thank you to the many prayer warriors and friends who asked how I was progressing.

Thank you to my husband Derek for giving me the freedom to pursue this project, and to review what I had written when I felt like I was nearly finished. My story of sudden suffering is his story also, since he was in the thick of it all. I didn't realize just how much he loved me until he was my caregiver, counselor, and best friend for those initial months of my physical limitation. Our marriage is better than it's ever been. We really did come through the difficulty, kinder, more patient, more loving, and with much more laughter.

Thank you to Alison who read the book many times at

differing stages. Her input and grammar helps are much appreciated. She encouraged and urged me to keep going. Thank you to Donna, who provided substantial input from her own vast experience in communication, and from writing several books herself. When I slowed down, she reminded me that it was God who gave me this work to do and that I needed to get it done!

Thank you to Holly, Jordyn, and Josie who all read parts of my book, and provided input. Thank you to David, for his advice on self-publishing. Thank you also to Alison, Donna, and Rob for their kind words about how this book impacted you. Thank you Owen and Abby at David & Brook Creative Agency who designed the cover, formatted my book, and prepared it for printing.

Finally, as I have said many times throughout this book, I thank Almighty God for what He did in and through my hardship, including giving me these words to share with others. To Him be the glory.

ABOUT THE AUTHOR

Wendy Stanley lives in Mount Forest with her husband and dog Sammy. Her passion is to encourage others, exhort the Scriptures, and to testify of the goodness of God by sharing her experiences as a follower of Jesus Christ. She's been writing blogs since November, 2013. This is her first book.

CPSIA information can be obtained
at www.ICGtesting.com
Printed in the USA
BVHW090035311222
655320BV00011B/1393